SARAH:
JOY IN THE MORNING

Sarah:
Joy in the Morning

The blessings of bereavement

Mary Cameron

Marshalls

Marshalls Paperbacks
Marshall Pickering
3 Beggarwod Lane, Basingstoke, Hants, RG23 7LP, UK
A subsidiary of the Zondervan Corporation

First published in 1985 by Marshall Morgan & Scott Ltd.

British Library CIP data

Cameron, Mary
  Sarah: joy in the morning
  1. Faith
  I. Title
  248.4 BT772

ISBN 0 551 01295 1

Typeset by Brian Robinson, North Marston, Bucks.
Printed in Great Britain by Hazel Watson & Viney,
Member of the BPCC Group, Aylesbury, Bucks.

*For Stephen, Rebecca and Hannah
and especially for Jenny.*

Acknowledgments

My thanks are due to so many people, without whose encouragement, faith and prayers, I would never have completed this book. In particular, my thanks to Betty, who typed the original manuscript and deciphered my writing so patiently; to Edward England, who so kindly read the original manuscript and whose comments on it gave me the necessary encouragement to try to find a publisher; to the hospital doctors who checked the medical details and were so enthusiastic about the book; to Father Matthew Jones, who offered many helpful suggestions and encouragement; and of course to Simon, whose story it is too, and whose practical support and encouragement has made this book possible.

Contents

The LORD says this:
> 'I myself will send an angel before you
> To guard you as you go and to bring you
> To the place that I have prepared.'

Exodus 23:20

Introduction

Wednesday, 29 December dawned like a spring day. It was very mild for late December, so mild, in fact, that we had the window open and outside birds were singing. The air was still. Inside the house, Stephen, Jenny, Rebecca and Hannah were all fast asleep, unaware that Simon and I were kneeling at Sarah's bedside. She was now deeply unconscious, her breathing faint and getting weaker. Sarah was dying.

Just before eight o'clock, her frail little body breathed its last faint breath and then, a moment or two later, her heart stopped. My hand had been resting on her chest and I had felt her heart racing, then slowing down until it was very slow and faint. 'Her heart's stopped,' I said. Dr Davidson, our consultant paediatrician, who had arrived a short while before, confirmed my words and nodded sadly in agreement. Hands reached down to comfort us, as Simon and I, still kneeling at Sarah's side remained motionless, completely stunned, devastated.

Then Dr Davidson and Lorraine, the nurse from the hospital who had accompanied him, quietly withdrew and left us on our own.

I shall never forget those moments: the sheer shock of death, though it was something we had known for some time was going to happen. Death, even when expected, is a tremendous shock, and our feelings of deepest sorrow and grief were at first numbed by this dreadful sense of shock, of disbelief even, that it really had happened.

In this book, I wanted to write of our own experience of facing death—the death of a nine-year-old daughter from leukaemia. It hasn't been easy to write. At times it has been just too painful, and my eyes have been too full of tears to write at all. But I have felt all the time a deep conviction that I should write, that I should share our experience, for although Sarah's death has brought us great sadness it has also brought us great joy.

I have wanted to show how a very ordinary family have struggled through an experience with which they would never have thought they could cope; an experience which in the eyes of many people is a tragedy: the loss and waste of a young life. But Sarah's death has not been a tragedy. It has been sad but through it we have received so many joys and blessings and it is these I want to share. Nor do we feel that her life has been wasted; on the contrary, in her short nine years Sarah has given so much.

A death such as Sarah's poses many questions: Is there a God at all? If there is, how can He allow children to die? How can He be kind and loving if He allows such things to happen?

We have found that there *is* a God, a God who loves us, and He is beside us all the way. I am so grateful to God for the way in which He has looked after us, and looking back it is beautiful to see how He has been helping us all the time.

We believe that Sarah's death was part of God's loving plan for us. It has opened our hearts and our lives to Him. We realised at the very beginning when Sarah first became ill, that we couldn't cope on our own. So we reached out to God for His help and He responded. He didn't take away the pain, the grief, the heartache; He didn't take away the tears, the sleepless nights, the brokenness we felt deep inside, but He did help us cope. He gave us His strength, a strength more powerful than we could have imagined. But more than that, He has increased our faith, He has given us new hope and a new awareness of His great love for us.

Sarah traces the last five months of Sarah's life. It tells of her illness and of her death, and of our feelings before and after her death. Our hope is that it will show how God has been looking after us all the time. Our experience has made us realise that God's love is more powerful and more wonderful than anything we could ever imagine, and that with God beside us we don't have to worry about anything. 'For I am certain that nothing can separate us from his love: neither death nor life, neither angels nor other heavenly rulers or powers, neither the present nor the future, neither the world above nor the world below—there is nothing in all creation that will ever be able to separate us from the love of God which is ours through Christ Jesus our Lord.' (Romans 8:38–39.)

How very reassuring and beautiful I have found this passage from St Paul. Nothing can separate us from the love of God. He loves us constantly, totally and eternally. Sarah's death has not separated us from His love; in fact it has done the opposite, it has brought us closer to Him, in a closeness we possibly would not have known any other way.

Isn't it true that sometimes you become closest to people when you have been through problems or difficulties and they have supported you, helped you, comforted you? We have found that with God. He has helped us so much and His love is a free gift for us all. It is not reserved for a few.

Through our great sadness in losing Sarah, we have discovered great joy. We have found peace, we have found love, we have found God. Yes, God does triumph over everything.

We have shared our feelings with many people and now I would like to share them with you too. Perhaps you have worries, problems, unhappiness. Maybe you, too, are experiencing the loss of someone you love; possibly like us, you have experienced the death of a child.

It is for you that I am writing this book. You may be so broken that you feel you can't cope, can't believe in a God at all, let alone in a kind God, a loving God. You may be bitter, resentful, angry. My prayer for you is that reading our story you, too, will reach out to God, for He *is* there and He will help you. Reach out to Him—you have nothing to lose, but so much to gain. From your brokenness, allow God to show you that He does love you and you, too, will receive His peace, His joy and His love.

1: 'Mrs Cameron, you have two lovely daughters'

There was nothing out of the ordinary about our family, apart from the fact that we had five children. We were living, and still do live, on a small farm in Gloucestershire. We had moved there just seven weeks before Jenny and Sarah, our twin daughters, were born. At the time, Stephen was a year old and I was completely unaware of the fact that I was carrying twins, although I was certainly much larger than I had been with Stephen.

The thought that I might be having twins had simply not dawned on me at all, although we did take out insurance when I was expecting Stephen, as one of my great-grandmothers had produced not just one but two sets of twins! But after Stephen's birth, we just didn't even think about the possibility of having twins.

I remember so clearly going to see the gynaecologist just two weeks before they were born. My doctor had sent me to see him because he thought the baby was in the breech position, that is turned round the opposite way from a normal delivery position. In these cases a doctor will often try to turn the baby round, as breech deliveries can sometimes present complications. My gynaecologist, however, examined me carefully and then said that he thought perhaps I should have an X-ray as he wasn't sure, but he thought that he could feel two heads. I gulped. 'You mean . . . you think that I might be going to have twins?' I asked. I was horrified. I wondered how on earth I would cope with twins. At that stage I was so tired, especially after having just moved, and I was finding it a full-time occupation looking after one baby of fourteen months, let alone two more!

Simon, too, was equally horrified when I arrived home with the news. But we talked about it (we certainly didn't pray about it) and, over the next few days, our initial shock subsided and we began to think that it would be rather exciting to have twins.

Five days after seeing my gynaecologist, Simon, Stephen and I drove over to Hereford for me to have an X-ray and by this time, far from dreading the possibility as had been my initial reaction, I would have been very disappointed if we had been told that it was only one baby after all. Simon, however, was still very apprehensive at the prospect. They told me the news right away and they even showed us the X-ray where you could very clearly see two little heads!

Jenny and Sarah were born ten days later by an emergency caesarian operation. That evening, Simon and I had put twenty pounds of carrots in the freezer and I had made an enormous quantity of faggots, which we had frozen. We had also, fortunately, done a huge shopping session that morning. It was almost as if some primitive maternal instinct was telling me that I was soon to give birth, so should lay in stores!

We got to bed quite late and round about two o'clock my waters suddenly broke and we woke up to a very wet bed. I felt absolutely fine with not even a twinge of a contraction, but nevertheless, as I had been told to do in such circumstances, I rang the hospital, who told me that I was definitely to come in. I even tried to persuade them to let me stay at home till the morning as I was so tired and all I wanted to do was go back to sleep. But, thank goodness, they insisted firmly that I should go in. If they hadn't, I very probably would have lost both babies.

Simon obviously couldn't take me in as it was the middle of the night and we didn't want to disturb Stephen, so we rang for an ambulance and I was soon being whisked off to the hospital, apologising profusely to the ambulance men for getting them up for nothing in the middle of the night. I felt like a complete fraud.

I was still apologising to the sister on duty at the hospital while she took down the usual information: name, address, religion etc. and I remember very clearly casually signing my name on the routine consent form in case of the need for an operation.

We were both joking and chatting and then the sister said that she should give me a routine examination, which she then set about doing. I shall never forget the look on her face. All colour simply drained out of it and she went completely white. But although she was obviously shocked and realised that something was very wrong indeed, she remained totally calm and I shall always be grateful to her for her prompt action and efficiency. Buzzers went, alarms rang, red lights flashed and before I knew what was happening I was being wheeled along on a trolley to the operating theatre. I asked what was wrong and was told that they would have to do a caesarian operation immediately. One of the babies' cords was actually coming out. 'I doubt very much if we can save the first baby,' the doctor told me, as I was being taken down to the theatre, 'but we'll certainly try to do what we can for the second.'

I was grateful for the relaxation exercises that I had been practising over the last few months and I consciously tried to relax, feeling that the less tense I was, the easier the doctor's job would be. And I also prayed, 'Dear God, please let them save one of the babies.'

We went straight in to the operating theatre. The doctor who was to do the operation had, in fact, been the one to help wheel me down on the trolley. To add to the pressures on the staff that night, not only did they have an emergency caesarian on their hands, but the porters were on strike, so the nursing staff themselves had taken me down to the operating theatre.

The last thing I was conscious of was a figure in green standing over me with a scalpel in his hand, and a nurse desperately trying to get a drip to go into my arm. She had to try several times but must have eventually succeeded because the next thing I knew was a sort of floating feeling as I was coming round from the anaesthetic and a voice that kept on repeating, 'Mrs Cameron, you have two lovely daughters.'

Jenny and Sarah had been born just minutes apart at 3.25 and 3.27 precisely, and only minutes after the initial alarm had been raised. We were so grateful to the magnificent hospital staff and we were thrilled to have two daughters!

The staff were as delighted as we were that they had managed to save both babies. It wasn't till later on that we discovered that I had had what is called a prolapsed cord, which is extremely serious. It means that the baby's cord has somehow come down, and in my case it was actually visible. That's why the sister had got such a shock. All I would have had to have done was to sit on it and that would have stopped the baby's heartbeat. Not only were the hospital staff delighted that we had two healthy babies, they were also amazed that they had been able to save them both, and while I was in hospital after their birth, several doctors and nurses came to see 'the mother with the prolapsed cord'.

Now, of course, we are even more grateful to have had two healthy daughters. Ironically, it was Jenny's life that the doctors then doubted that they could save. How even more grateful we are now, that they were able to do so.

The girls seemed tiny to us and their little arms and legs were no bigger than Simon's fingers but in fact, they were good weights at 4 pounds 8 ounces and 4 pounds 13 ounces, Sarah being the heavier of the two. I was determined to breast feed them even though I didn't have very much milk, but my determination and perseverance paid off, as in the end I fed them both for nearly nine months.

I stayed in the hospital for two weeks and the worst thing was being away from Stephen who was still only a baby himself, so it was wonderful to come home and be with Simon and Stephen, and eat fresh homegrown vegetables, drink our own fresh milk and sleep in my own bed. Jenny and Sarah stayed in the hospital for another week until they were a little bit bigger so during that time I expressed my milk for them. By the end of the week, I was beginning to feel a bit like a cow! But each evening, Simon and I drove to the hospital taking the daily offering of milk in a huge Kilner jar, which became quite a joke with the hospital staff. 'Here comes United Dairies,' they would say, on seeing us arrive each evening!

We were soon able to bring the girls home and then began the hard work, but also the fun, of looking after them and Stephen and, of course, the farm too.

2: A move to Gloucestershire

We love our small farm, situated in beautiful countryside on the Gloucestershire/Herefordshire borders. We are lucky enough to have thirty acres of mainly pasture land and a small cider apple orchard, which is beautiful in the spring time with its apple and pear blossom. The fields in spring are full of lovely little wild daffodils and primroses, and the woods around us are a carpet of flowers.

Our house itself is an old cottage-type farmhouse. Built in the late sixteenth, or early seventeenth century, it is not a house for anyone over six foot tall as it is full of low ceilings and low beams.

We are so lucky to be living in such a lovely house and the way in which we found the house itself was also remarkable. In fact, it seemed from the very beginning that we were meant to live there.

Simon and I had originally both been brought up in Hertfordshire. I was the eldest of six children; Simon was an only child. We had both been to boarding schools and Simon then went to agricultural college for a time before going to work on a mushroom farm in Essex. I had spent a year abroad working with families in France and Austria, learning the languages, before going to teacher training college, and it was just before I started my first teaching job that Simon and I first met.

We met in a pub, introduced by a mutual friend. Simon was living at home and driving over to Essex each day to work and I had intended sharing a flat with two friends in London, where I was teaching. But as Simon and I were soon seeing each other every day, my idea of a flat in London was shelved and I decided to stay at home and commute into London each day instead.

We soon realised that our friendship was far more than a casual romance, and very soon decided that we wanted to spend the rest of our lives with each other. A year after our first meeting we became engaged and we were married five months later.

We moved into the small lodge house on the mushroom farm and were extremely happy. I was teaching in a local infant school, which I loved, and Simon was busy on the farm. I carried on teaching until just before Stephen was born and we found our new role as parents brought us even closer together.

After Stephen's birth, we started looking for a house of our own. We hoped to find something with a little bit of land, where Simon intended to start his own small mushroom farm.

We looked at properties in Norfolk but then decided that as there were already several very large mushroom farms in that area, we would be better off elsewhere. Then we just happened to stay overnight in Ledbury en route to Wales for a few days holiday, and we both immediately fell in love with the area. On studying the map, we discovered that it was ideally situated with several large and other smaller markets within easy reach. This persuaded us to try to find something in the area, so I wrote off to literally dozens of estate agents within a fifty mile radius.

Weeks went by and, although we had looked at several places, nothing suitable had come up. We were starting to get slightly desperate. Firstly, we had hoped to find a house and move before Christmas and secondly and far more important, we had discovered that I was pregnant and were therefore most anxious to move before the arrival of another baby.

In September, when I was four months pregnant and already fairly huge, we found a property that seemed a possibility, though it wasn't exactly what we had been looking for. It was a modern three-bedroomed house on an existing five acre market garden. The market garden was highly efficient and productive but we didn't really want an existing market garden, nor did we really want a modern house. We had dreamed of finding a lovely old farmhouse with lots of beams and a huge old farmhouse kitchen. One of my ambitions had always been to have a house cow and I could just imagine a big kitchen with an enormous table in the middle where everyone could gather, and where I could make butter and homemade bread.

However, we decided that although the property we had found wasn't exactly what we had been looking for, it would be sensible to move before the birth of our next baby and at least it would give us a start. We could always move again at a later date. So we made an offer and were accepted.

However, two weeks later we were gazumped, which we were quite unprepared for. We were disappointed at the time but certainly, looking back, it was a blessing in disguise. We decided not to raise our original offer but instead to start looking for properties all over again, although this was a depressing thought.

We were still recovering from our disappointment when two days later we had a phone call from an estate agent in Ledbury. He had news of a property that wasn't actually yet on the market. He described it over the phone: 'Small kitchen, large sitting room and hall downstairs . . . three bedrooms and a bathroom upstairs . . . thirty acres of land'. He was very enthusiastic about it and wanted us to come and have a look at it, but I pointed out that the house sounded rather small and thirty acres of land was far too much. Fortunately, he was not deterred by my lack of interest and said that he would post the details to us, and asked if we would at least consider coming to have a look at it. I told him that it really did sound out of the question, but he could send the details if he liked.

The details arrived in the morning post and no sooner had we read about the beams in the house and the old farm buildings, and the cider house complete with cider press than we were on the phone ourselves saying that it sounded fantastic and that we definitely wanted to come and see it, and when was the soonest we could come?

The minute we walked down the path leading to the house and saw the tubs full of flowers, the black and white barn and the whitewashed old cottage, we knew that it was right for us. We were met at the door by the elderly lady who lived in the house, who told us at once that she didn't really want to sell at all. But she kindly showed us around all the same. It was exactly what we had always dreamed of: huge beams, old quarry tile floors, beautiful old doors, a big open fireplace in the sitting room, a walk-in larder and a concreted farmyard surrounded by lovely old farm buildings. Miss B., we were told, had lived in the house for over fifty years with her family and she was one of ten children. We couldn't imagine where they had all slept as one of the three bedrooms had originally been a barn and had only recently been converted into a bedroom. Miss B. herself had been running the farm singlehanded ever since the death of her father a few years previously. Her main activity was rearing calves, which she then sold to the local market, but she was now having eye trouble and thought that she might move.

We told her how much we liked the house, and I am sure that the fact that we had Stephen with us, who was by then a gorgeous nine-month-old baby, and that my bump by this stage was fairly large, must have been in our favour, for when we returned home, we made an offer for the property, which to our great delight was accepted.

We moved the following January. On our arrival Miss B. was there to greet us with a huge log fire blazing in the sitting room, and coffee brewing in the kitchen. She had left us all the carpets and curtains and even soap and hand towels, as well as potatoes, onions and eggs in the store room. And we had bought her fifteen hens, complete with hen house.

We were so touched by her wonderful warm welcome to us, more like one would have expected from one's grand-mother than from a comparative stranger. In fact, when Jenny and Sarah were born she wrote us the most beautiful letter welcoming the girls to the old house. We felt as if we had really come home.

We were so grateful to have found and moved into our lovely old house and to have everything work out so well. How strange it seemed to think that we hadn't even been interested in the house when we first heard about it over the phone. Thank goodness the estate agent was so persistent—and how lucky too that the house was never on the open market, and that we had been gazumped on the other house.

I believed then, and believe even more so now, that nothing happens by chance. And although I am sure that I thanked God for our house, I certainly was not sure then as I am now that He is leading and guiding us all the way. Now I would say that it was part of God's unfolding plan for us to move into that particular house, in that particular area and at that particular time. Although we didn't realise it, God was very quietly starting to make His presence and His love known to us.

3: Life on the farm

We settled into our new life and were extremely happy. Then came the birth of the girls and, around the same time, Simon started to grow some vegetables on about four acres of ground to give us an income while he built the mushroom farm. That first summer was pretty hectic with looking after two babies and a toddler and helping on the market garden. I shall always remember Simon and I each pushing a pram down to the field with Stephen very often perched on one of them for the ride. Then Simon and I would attempt to plant lettuces with two little babies shrieking from their prams at the side of the field, while Stephen with his bucket and spade would dig the lettuce plants up almost as quickly as we planted them!

Meanwhile, we had bought our first Jersey house cow and Simon soon became proficient at milking her and I learnt how to skim the cream and make butter, yoghurt and cottage cheese. The milk and cream itself is delicious and we are very lucky always having plenty. We had adopted a way of life that is much envied by many people: we were fairly self-sufficient, producing all our own dairy products, growing our own vegetables and producing some of our own meat too, for we also keep a few sheep and a couple of pigs. We make our own wine and in those days I made all our own bread, too.

It's a great life for the children who benefit from plenty of space and fresh air and the fact that Simon is always somewhere nearby. They often accompany Simon on his morning or evening rounds of feeding the animals, and even the youngest can help in some way. The milking is done by hand and they all love standing and watching while this is being done. It is also lovely for the children when we have baby calves, piglets and lambs. They have all seen these baby animals being born and have witnessed the miracle of nature as a newborn calf struggles to its feet only minutes after being born.

While starting the market garden, Simon also started building the mushroom farm, which consisted of seven plastic growing sheds, just like ordinary plastic tunnels except these were covered with two layers of black polythene and the two layers were sandwiched together with a layer of fibreglass for insulation. He also had a huge open barn constructed to use for mixing up the compost and filling the growing boxes.

The mushroom farm went into production and it was very exciting. It did, however, take up more and more of Simon's time but, like most people who are starting up their own business, we made it our primary concern. The mushrooms were delicious and we sold them to local markets with no trouble. In fact there seemed to be quite a demand for them and people soon started coming to buy them at the farm and we built up a good door trade. We even produced mushroom recipe leaflets which we gave away free with a box of mushrooms.

Then things started to go wrong. Oil prices soared and, as Simon was dependent on a constant supply of oil to heat the growing sheds, this hit us badly. Then wages went up and, as we had five full-time people working on the farm, this again was bad news for us. In the end, like so many other small growers, we were forced to give up. So we concentrated on the market garden, growing beans, lettuces, courgettes, sweetcorn and cabbages. The plastic mushroom growing sheds have been converted into tunnels where we grow tomatoes, cucumbers, peppers and aubergines.

We utilised the door trade that had arisen from the mushrooms and started a small farm shop, selling mostly in the summer months. The bulk of our produce still went to local markets and we also delivered to a few local shops.

We were very happy although we led a hectic, busy life devoting all our time and energies to the market garden and to the children, though in the summer months certainly more time went to the market garden than to the children.

In the winter months however, when things weren't quite so hectic, Simon did manage to do quite a few projects in and around the house and spend more time with the family. His biggest project by far has been a magnificent new kitchen extension which has enlarged our house considerably and has given us the lovely big farmhouse kitchen we had always dreamed of. It is basically very simple with a huge six foot pine table in the middle where I make bread and butter, where the children paint, draw or do cookery, and of course it is the most wonderful place for us to gather, as a family or with our friends, over a cup of coffee or a bottle of wine.

Time passed and Stephen and the girls grew. They went to playgroup and then started school. I shall never forget that first day when Jenny and Sarah went to school for the first time. I was so lonely without them. Sarah was then getting a lot of headaches, especially when she was tired, so she went for mornings only to begin with, which Jenny didn't mind at all. They were so very different, Sarah having less energy than Jenny and also being much more of a home-bird whereas Jenny loved school from the very beginning.

Simon and I both developed minor illnesses. Mine was a glandular disease that made me incredibly tired and also affected my eyes, with the result that I needed eye treatment and frequent checkups at the eye hospital for several years. Simon developed rheumatoid arthritis, which fortunately didn't last long but necessitated a couple of stays in hospital, and also having his entire leg in a plaster cast for twelve weeks. Apart from being very painful, it was awful for Simon who was so active to become suddenly immobile. He did plant broad beans with his walking stick, literally hobbling down the field to do so—but, far more important, he started making baskets.

Simon's basketmaking, which started as a hobby, has now become a winter enterprise. His beautiful willow baskets have got better and better—he makes all sorts: log baskets, shopping baskets of different shapes and sizes, children's baskets. So again, something which to start with seemed disastrous has ended up by being a blessing in disguise, for I am sure that if Simon had not had his leg in plaster for so long he would never have started making baskets.

Simon makes his baskets in a room at one end of the house, originally the store room. Next to it is the old dairy which is now my pottery, where I have a kick wheel and where, when I can, I sit and throw pots. I am very much of an amateur but after cookery it is my favourite pastime. I also have a small electric kiln so I can fire my own pots. This is lovely for the children too as they enjoy making something with clay and often join me when I am potting.

When Jenny and Sarah were six, Rebecca was born. It was lovely to have a little baby in the house again and after the experience of three so close together, it seemed incredibly easy to have one baby on its own. Stephen and the girls all adored their baby sister and I was never short of willing helpers. They soon all became very good at changing nappies, and enjoyed pushing Rebecca in her pram or just playing with her.

Hannah was born two and a half years later and again it was wonderful for us as a family to share looking after another new baby. In fact with four willing helpers this time and Simon keen to spend time with her too, I'm sure that if I hadn't been breast feeding I would nearly have been made redundant!

Stephen was now ten and a half, tall, with blond hair and blue eyes. He was extremely practical, like his father, enjoyed woodwork and often helped Simon with jobs around the farm. He enjoyed helping me in the kitchen and was becoming a very good cook. He was also keen on sport, especially cricket, and liked riding his bike and watching television.

With Stephen having four sisters and especially twin sisters so close to him in age, and with us living a rather isolated life in the countryside, we began to think that it was important for Stephen to be around other boys and have the opportunity to pursue and develop his love of sport. We decided to send him as a weekly boarder to a school about eighteen miles away, which had impressed us with its warm family atmosphere and the genuine friendliness of both children and staff, and the fact that everyone seemed happy there and obviously worked hard and played hard. Stephen settled in very quickly and has thrived and blossomed in the happy and stimulating atmosphere. As he is a weekly boarder, it means of course that Stephen isn't at home from Monday to Friday, but this is compensated for by the fact that he comes home for Saturday and Sunday nights, so we do have the weekend together as a family and, during the week, time that would otherwise be spent on travelling can be used for all sorts of other activities.

Jenny and Sarah were nine and not a bit like twins really. Some people did muddle them up occasionally but their similarities were not so much from being twins as from being sisters. In fact, the family likeness of all the children has always been particularly noticeable and people have often remarked to us how very similar they all are in looks.

Jenny was the darkest of the family with darkish brown hair and hazel eyes. She was very artistic, musical and fond of all outdoor pursuits. She too enjoyed riding her bike, swimming, skipping, and netball and P.E. at school. She was an avid reader and a very fast one.

Sarah was very like Stephen in looks with blond hair and blue eyes, slighter in build than Jenny but the same height. Unlike Jenny, she was not very 'sporty' although she did enjoy swimming. They were both intelligent and went to the same school where, although they were in the same class, they very often played with different friends. Sarah had several good friends but Jenny had one special friend, also called Sarah, who became and remained her 'best' friend all during the school.

We were pleased that they did, in fact, have separate friends of their own. From the very beginning, we felt that it was important for them as twins to develop and retain their own identity as much as possible and we rarely, if at all, ever referred to them as twins. However it was super for them to grow up with a playmate always there and to have that special sort of friendship that only twins can experience. Even when they were babies, they enjoyed each other's company. They were far less bored than a single baby is, as they always had each other for company. They used to entertain each other, giggle with each other and just be content to be together when they were in their prams in the garden, and as they grew up they became very close friends.

At home, they both enjoyed cooking, playing with their dolls, drawing, reading and making up games together. They were both learning to play the piano and were both Brownies. In fact, that summer, before Sarah became ill, they both went on their Brownie pack holiday for the first time. The pack usually went to a farm not too far away from us, where there is plenty of space and the overriding attraction is a huge outdoor swimming pool!

Both Jenny and Sarah had really been looking forward to their pack holiday and had a fantastic time. Jenny settled in with hardly a thought about leaving us for a week, but Sarah was very homesick, even though she had Jenny and several close friends with her. However, it certainly didn't spoil her week, though she was overjoyed to be back home with us at the end of the week.

I suppose that, of the two of them, Jenny was the more independent and also the more self-reliant. Although they were very close, if, for instance, one of them went to play with a friend, Jenny could cope much better than Sarah with being without her twin.

Sarah was extremely tidy, whereas Jenny was not. Sarah too was very conscientious and worried about things more than Jenny did. Jenny, although sensitive, was more happy-go-lucky. She achieved things with considerable ease and far more quickly than Sarah did and was, outwardly at least, the more confident of the two.

Sarah herself was a warm affectionate child. She was full of compassion for others, particularly those worse off than herself. She never liked anyone spending a lot of money on her. She would save everything. If they were given some sweets, Sarah never ate all of hers, but saved some and shared them out at a later date, very often to console someone who was feeling unhappy. She was easy to talk to, she had a lovely sense of humour, and above all was incredibly kind and very patient, particularly with her younger sisters. She adored looking after them and was a super little 'nanny'.

Sarah loved being at home and would have been quite happy not going to school at all! She had had her share of illnesses, the normal childhood earaches and infections, but she also suffered from migraine headaches. We discovered that chocolate and also pork sometimes seemed to bring these on. So she stopped eating those foods, although it really hurt her sometimes when the others ate chocolate. She also seemed to get migraines from over-tiredness or worry and frequently missed odd days of school because of this. She had also had three eye operations for a squint, so she had already become familiar with hospitals.

An idea of Sarah's character can be gained from what my brother Paul, who is a doctor, wrote to us in a letter the day she died:

It was wonderful to see Sarah the day Tony and I came over from Oxford—despite obvious ill-health, her very special character, intelligence, and sense of fun shone through. In my short time in paediatrics I have come across a few children who really do stand out from the rest. They are the ones who never complain, however often we stick needles into them, they are always cheerful and their indifference to suffering and the maturity of their attitude to their own disease would do credit to many a sick adult! Sarah struck me as being just such a child, one could not help but like her.

Yes, it was her cheerfulness and her sense of fun that made her so very special. In the photographs we have of Sarah she is nearly always smiling!

Rebecca was then three and a half. She too had blond hair and blue eyes and was very similar in looks to both Sarah and Stephen. Rebecca simply adored Sarah, whom she called 'Herry', and loved playing with her. In a way, I suppose, she looked upon Sarah as a sort of mother figure. Sarah had incredible patience with her and Rebecca also had great respect for Sarah. Very often Sarah could get her to do something she didn't particularly want to do with the minimum of fuss. Rebecca loved playing outside, digging in the sandpit and helping Simon with the animals. She also spent hours playing with her dolls, very often with Sarah.

Rebecca's special friend was a little boy of the same age, called James who went to the same playgroup. His parents, Anne and Russell, were special friends of ours. When Sarah became ill they were to become even closer, and it was they who looked after the children when we had to be in the hospital with Sarah. Sarah and their middle son, Daniel, had a very special friendship. Although Sarah was three years older than Daniel they just seemed to click and they were very fond of each other.

Hannah was a gorgeous cuddly baby. Everyone adored looking after her and she was quite used to being handed around for one or other of the children to look after her or play with her. She was an extremely happy baby and very easy. Our only problem with her was that she didn't sleep very well at night, but she was so happy the rest of the time, and we had become so used to broken nights that we didn't worry about it. We knew she would grow out of it in time.

In the days before Sarah became ill, we led a hectic, busy life, devoting all our time and attention to the market garden and the children. Growing vegetables is hard work and Simon worked extremely hard—sometimes getting up as early as 4 a.m. to cut lettuces and working all through the day, not finishing till 10 p.m. We loved our children but rarely spent much time together as a family, particularly in the summertime. The farm was invariably the most important thing, so even at the weekends, Simon worked.

We were extremely happy, however, and incredibly lucky. We certainly didn't appreciate quite how lucky we were and our values then were different than they are now.

We were continually worried about overdrafts, farm mortgages, bank charges and so on. Our main aim in life was to run a successful business and, although we weren't really materialistic and certainly didn't want to change our fairly simple lifestyle, we hoped to be able to make a reasonable profit and lead a comfortable sort of life.

The one thing missing in our married life was, and always had been, the fact that Simon and I lacked shared religious beliefs or ideas. I had been brought up as a Roman Catholic,

Simon in the Church of England. My religion has always been important to me and I was sad that this was the one thing that I could not share with Simon. We rarely talked about religion at all and if we did, we usually only argued. However, we respected each other's different ideas. And although Simon didn't come to church with me except very occasionally, he had no objection to my going, nor to bringing the children up as Catholics.

Simon just didn't see the point of going to church. He felt that one could lead a perfectly good Christian life without ever going inside a church. In fact the whole idea of going to church seemed rather hypocritical to him. He didn't really feel a great need for God in his life. Like so many men, he was the breadwinner, the father, the husband, the one looked to for help if something went wrong and he was managing perfectly well fulfilling these roles without God. We were fairly self-sufficient and self-reliant. We coped with minor problems on our own. And we were also happy, so we didn't really question the fundamental issues of life at all. We were much too busy looking after our farm and our children to worry about such questions as: Why are we here? What should we be doing with our lives? What happens when we die? We just lived our life, I suppose, placing our priorities on the farm and the children. We hadn't come face to face with anything which had made us think any differently. So we didn't really think very much about life. We certainly never thought about death.

Simon and I never prayed together, nor did we pray as a family, although Simon or I would say bedtime prayers with each child as we tucked them up at night. We would have called ourselves a Christian family, meaning that we tried to live a Christian way of life, but in doing so, we were, in fact, placing the emphasis on the way of life that we were leading, not on who was leading us. Now, we would view the whole idea of being a Christian as putting Jesus Christ first in one's life, placing the emphasis on Him, rather than on the actual way of life we lead.

So, although we called ourselves Christians, our ideas were to change. For me, God was not the very real person that He has now become, nor was He the central part of my life. I wasn't really committed as a Christian. Yes, I was a practising Catholic but in those days, my religion meant that I thought I should be trying to do something for God. I didn't realise that I can do absolutely nothing for God unless I allow Him to do something for me, unless I allow Him into my heart and into my life, unless I place Him first in my life and allow Him to be Lord of my life. I had to allow God to do the changing. Like the clay on the potter's wheel, we need to allow God to mould us and it is only by allowing God to change us that we can do anything at all for Him.

We were both to change, Simon perhaps even more dramatically than me. And gradually we both came to realise that religion isn't just going to church, nor is it imposed rules and authority, but it is a beautiful, living relationship with a loving God and it is Good News!

4: Angela

The market garden grew and we were always looking for better ways of selling our vegetables. Encouraged by the door trade that had built up when we had been growing mushrooms, and finding that the market price for vegetables was sometimes so low that it was hardly even worthwhile picking them, we had started selling vegetables at the door and soon built up a flourishing 'farm shop'. Some vegetables, including tomatoes and runner beans, we sold on a pick-your-own basis. Simon picked other vegetables each day and we arranged these for sale in his lovely willow baskets, in our large barn. We also sold bunches of dried flowers we had grown, pots of herbs, petunias and strings of onions and garlic. We had a huge blackboard on the wall with prices chalked up on it. Everything was very simple, very fresh and all home grown.

We advertised in local papers and had a fairly steady stream of customers, particularly at the weekends, when it was sometimes so busy that our large concrete yard was crammed full of cars.

To start with, we managed everything on our own but it became more and more difficult to cope with the selling, the picking and looking after the children especially as our busiest selling time coincided with the summer holidays. The weekends were the busiest of course and it got to the stage that sometimes the farm shop was so busy that I couldn't leave even to fix a meal, so one way and another the children were starting to suffer. It was then that we decided to find a young girl, a sort of mother's help, who could live with us as part of our family and be another pair of hands, wherever and whenever needed.

For the last few summers we had found suitable girls. It seemed to work quite successfully and meant that I could do some of the selling knowing that there was someone in the house looking after the children, and I could be free to look after the children too. It also meant that if I was in the middle of making bread, as so often had happened, with my hands full of dough and flour, I didn't have to wash my hands, pick up the children and dash over to the farm every time someone came for vegetables, as there was someone else who could do so. This really was a marvellous help and even more so because the time of building up the farm shop also coincided with the two and a half years that saw the births of Rebecca and Hannah, when we were even more grateful for an extra pair of hands.

We hadn't thought about finding anyone for the summer of 1982 but then we were told by a friend of a friend about an American girl called Angela who wanted to live with a family, preferably with children and on a farm, and she wondered if we were interested. We said that we would be, but then discovered that Angela wanted a family by May, which was really far too early on in the year for us, as July to September were our busiest months. However, we agreed to meet Angela and we were so pleased that we did!

She came and chatted to us over a cup of tea in our kitchen. We liked her instantly and just had a feeling that she was meant to come to us, even if May was a bit early. She said that she was keen to do anything and would help us in any way she could. She also promised to see if she could stay till the end of August. She phoned a few weeks later to say that she could only stay until the beginning of July, but *please* could she come, she would be happy to come for nothing and even sleep in the hay! So we agreed that she should come at the beginning of May.

It is fantastic to look back and see how God was looking after us all. By sending Angela to us, he provided us with the extra help we needed, so that when Sarah became ill in July we were not as tired as we normally would have been by then. We all loved having Angela with us. She was such fun, great company and a fantastic worker. She happily got up to pack lettuces with Simon at 4 a.m., then she would muck out the cow-sheds, do the hardest and dirtiest jobs and in between-times, she would hoe like mad and then pop into the kitchen, clear up, lay the table, rock Hannah to sleep and rustle up the most delicious brownies and flapjacks! Her energy seemed boundless and she was one of the most cheerful people I have ever met. It did us all the power of good having her with us.

Angela in her turn seemed delighted to be with us. She adored the children and got on really well with Simon and me. In fact we became very close friends. She was a very warm, sincere person and fitted in right away as one of the family. Occasionally in life, you do meet someone with whom you are immediately relaxed and just seem to 'hit it off' as if you have known them for ages. It was just like that with Angela and us. Furthermore, she was a vegetarian! So she was thrilled to be able to eat masses of our fresh vegetables all the time and we were equally thrilled to have such an appreciative house guest, and one who didn't want to eat lots of meat!

Halfway during Angela's stay with us, we had another house guest, this time an eighteen-year-old French boy called Hugues. I had spent some time with Hugues' family in France when I had left school, when Hugues himself was only a baby! But he was now at agricultural college in France and wanted to live with an English family for a few weeks in the summer, improving his English and helping out on a farm. Hence his visit to us. And how kind God was to organise extra help for us when again we didn't know we were going to need it, because after Angela left and Sarah became ill, it was marvellous to have Hugues, who could and did help on the farm whenever needed, especially when Simon was in the hospital. Also the children adored him and he was great with them too. Being one of six children, he was quite used to large families. He even got on well with little Hannah and so if Simon wasn't at home, Hugues would often have a game of football with Stephen or read a story to the little ones and just the presence of another caring person in the house was good for all of us.

We were also fortunate in having Mark, a sixteen-year-old local boy, who was working full time for Simon on the farm. Without him, we certainly wouldn't have managed. He coped with Simon's frequent and often sudden departures magnificently and we were very grateful for his loyalty, conscientiousness and hard work.

Sadly, Angela had to leave us on 12 July. The weekend before, we decided to have a party, a sort of 4 July celebration. We gave it a theme: '60s—Come as you were' and everyone dressed accordingly. Some people really went to town with mini-skirts, flower-power, and Beatles and Stones regalia! It was great fun. We emptied our playroom at one end of the house, to make it available for dancing and Simon dug out all our old Beatles and Stones records. People also brought their own favourite 'golden oldies' of the '60s. It was, fortunately, a beautiful evening, so apart from the dancing, we were outside for most of the evening.

We all had great fun dressing for the party. Even Stephen and the girls dressed up. The girls wore their pretty summer bridesmaid dresses with flowers in their hair and Stephen wore jeans and an old jeans jacket which he had fun decorating. Simon found a baggy white shirt to go with his jeans and a brightly coloured flowery scarf, and I found a mini dress and lots of beads!

As it was the middle of the summer, we had plenty of vegetables growing, so Angela and I made lots of different salads and also some puddings and everyone brought something to drink. We all really enjoyed both the preparation and the party itself and it was specially nice that Stephen, Jenny and Sarah were able to join in with us.

At this time, I had become aware that Sarah wasn't looking too well. She had a lot of bruises on her legs and a few tiny little purple spots on her body. We didn't think much about it but the week after our party, she got steadily worse. It was very hot and each afternoon at school, they were practising for the Sports Day. When Sarah came home she complained of feeling tired and towards the end of the week had several nose-bleeds at school. I put these down to the hot weather, but afterwards felt terribly guilty that I had made her go to school at all. I am rather soft and if any of the children aren't too well I keep them at home—or usually did. Anyway, I was trying to be less soft, so I sent her to school each day. It makes me shudder now to think of it.

However, when Sarah came back from school on Friday, I decided she would not go back until she had been to the doctor and so made an appointment for her on the following Tuesday morning. On Monday, Angela was leaving and we were taking her to Cheltenham to catch her coach. I really don't know how we could have been so ignorant, but we just thought that Sarah was anaemic, as she was, but not for the usual reasons. I tried to think of tempting sources of iron, but she just wasn't interested in eating. We then realised how pale and thin she was. She was very irritable too, not like Sarah at all, normally the most patient and tolerant of us all. She was also terribly tired.

On Monday, we took Angela to catch her coach. By now, Sarah's stomach was hurting and she found it painful to walk. We later found out that her spleen was very enlarged and this was causing the pain. I was grateful to get Sarah home and tuck her up in bed and even more grateful that we would be seeing the doctor in the morning. That night, I slept in Sarah's bed with her. As I lay next to her, I was aware of a strange feeling. I felt that I was close to a child who was very seriously ill, dying even. I dismissed the idea at once. That night, Sarah had a dreadful nose-bleed, it just would not stop, and of course I had no idea at the time why it wouldn't stop. After a very long time and with the help of ice-packs and rolls of tissues, it finally ceased and Sarah went to sleep.

5: Be still and know that I am God

Our doctor's appointment on Tuesday morning was fairly early and for some reason, rather than take Sarah on my own, I asked Simon to come with us. He was very busy but agreed to take us, and how grateful I was that he did. The minute Dr Sims looked at Sarah his face showed that this was very serious indeed. He examined her gently, took a sample of blood, and then sent us both outside. I took Sarah out to sit in the car with Simon and went back in to see Dr Sims on my own. I was trembling—I seemed to be quite cold. Then he said, 'I'm afraid it's serious.'

'Yes, I know,' I said.

'I can't be absolutely sure, but I feel it's only fair to tell you, I think Sarah has leukaemia.' Stunned silence—I couldn't speak—I had known all along. How, why, I don't know, but I had known.

'I don't know why, but I thought it was leukaemia,' I said.

'She'll have to go to hospital right away. They'll do some tests to confirm it, but it's certainly right on top of the list of possibilities. I *am* sorry.'

I burst into tears, apologised, blowing my nose, 'Simon's in the car, we'd better tell him,' I said. Dr Sims sent a nurse out to sit with the children and broke the news to Simon, who like me was horrified and shaken and then broke down into tears.

We tried to ring a friend to look after the two little ones, who were also with us, but because we were unable to contact her we decided we would go to Gloucester together. We knew we couldn't tell Sarah, or let her know anything was wrong, so we tried to be as cheerful as possible and announced that we were going to Gloucester to the hospital so they could do some tests. She happily cuddled up next to me. She was feeling so ill, and we were full of apprehension and shock. I prayed as we drove to the hospital. It all seemed like a bad dream.

On arrival at the hospital, Sarah was immediately admitted. She was put into a single room with windows all along two sides, which looked out into the ward and along the corridor. She had blood tests and X-rays and was immediately put on a drip. Simon and I took it in turns to stay with her and look after Hannah and Rebecca.

Sarah was to have a bone marrow test that afternoon—necessitating a general anaesthetic. It seemed forever that we all waited out in the garden. We were so stunned still. All we could do was hope and pray. We rang a very good friend and asked her if she would meet Jenny from her school bus, and Simon would collect her later while I stayed in the hospital with Sarah.

The consultant paediatrician, Dr Davidson, wanted to have a chat with us both. We went into his little office, where Hannah fortunately fell asleep in my arms. Dr Davidson was very kind. He explained that Sarah had acute lymphoblastic leukaemia, and that it was treatable. What they planned to do was to try to get her into 'remission' with very strong drugs, knocking out all the leukaemic cells. She was very anaemic and needed blood which they would also give her, with some platelets, as her platelet count was so low—that was why she was bruising and had all the nose-bleeds.

'Is she going to die?' I asked. 'Well, she has a fifty-fifty chance,' the doctor replied. He added that probably most of what he had said wouldn't really sink in, so we were very welcome to have another talk at any time, or ask any questions we wanted. I think the fact that Sarah had a chance gave us a tremendous boost and made us very hopeful. Leukaemia certainly seemed to be far more treatable than we had thought and both Simon and I tended naturally to look on the hopeful, brighter side. The main thing at the moment was that she could be brought into remission and we both prayed that this would happen.

On the practical side, because of the animals at home and the market garden, we decided that Simon should return home and I was to stay with Sarah overnight. However, as I was breast feeding Hannah, I would obviously have to keep her with me. The hospital staff were very helpful and found a huge pram for Hannah which just fitted into one corner of Sarah's room, but with the drips and stands there wasn't too much space! My bed was a roll-down chair which was in fact very comfortable, although in the next few days I was to get so little sleep that I would have been happy with the floor!

Little Hannah was no trouble at all, though she hadn't been sleeping too well at home and this was no time for her to be waking up at night—so I did start giving her a sedative, on the doctor's advice. Sarah's drugs were given intravenously through her drip every two hours, but one lot of drugs had to be given very slowly, and they stung as they went in—sometimes they were extremely painful. Because of all her extra fluid intake she also needed to be put on a bedpan very frequently, so what with that and being woken for her drugs every two hours, neither of us got very much sleep that first night. However, I was so grateful to be there, close to her, and only wanted to be with her and help her in any way possible.

The next few days were some of the worst for us all. We, of course, had family and friends whom we had to tell of Sarah's illness. They were all shocked initially, but we were glad that we could reassure them that leukaemia *can* be treatable and that Sarah was getting first class medical care and nursing. My father, on hearing the news, flew over from the Isle of Man the next day with a friend—to run the house for us, cook, clean and look after the children which was really a marvellous help. I don't know how we could have managed otherwise.

Obviously we had to tell both Sarah and the other children what was wrong with her, and so we truthfully told them that she had leukaemia, which meant that there was something wrong with her blood. We were always completely honest with them, but strangely enough, although they were all very interested about the disease and its treatment and we answered all their questions perfectly straightforwardly, the question 'Was she going to die?' never arose and none of the children realised that the disease could be fatal, for which we were very relieved.

The next day Simon came in twice to visit Sarah, and the next and the next. We were both very tired and completely drained emotionally too. On one of his visits, we decided he should stay with Sarah on his own and I could push Hannah into the town. I needed a few things and the fresh air would do us both good. As we set off my eyes were full of tears and I prayed for strength. We reached a busy road and my legs felt like jelly—'I can't go on, I'll turn back,' I thought for a moment. But I became determined to go on, and as I crossed the busy road and saw all the hordes of shoppers, it suddenly struck me so forcibly that we are all going to die one day, when our time comes. We don't know when or how. Yes, Sarah has leukaemia, she could die, but so could any of us get knocked over by a bus tomorrow. We can't worry about what is going to happen to us, we must just take each day as it comes, trusting that God knows what is best for us. He is there by our side, helping us each step of the way.

Thinking like this, I suddenly saw clearly how Angela's coming to us had been part of God's plan. He had, of course, known all along that we would need to have special help before Sarah became ill, so that we would be physically strong enough to cope with the extra demands that were now being put on us. Angela had been such a help to both Simon and me. Normally by mid-summer, Simon is pretty shattered having been working seven days a week nearly non-stop, with not much sleep, but having had an extra pair of hands had kept him from being as tired as he normally gets. I was still feeding an eight-month-old baby when Angela first arrived, and looking after four other children as well, so for me another pair of hands was a fantastic help. Furthermore, Angela herself was such a special person, so full of love and joy, and so those few months she spent with us were a very joyful time for us all. Yes, God had most definitely included Angela in His plan for us, to prepare us, in a way, so that we would be able to cope.

Realising that God had already been helping us, without us even knowing about it at the time, gave me great trust that if He was looking after us when we didn't even realise we needed it and hadn't asked for it, He would even more certainly be looking after us now that we realised that we did need His help, and were asking for it.

I felt so much happier and more peaceful than I had felt since Sarah's illness was diagnosed. Of course all we can do is trust in God, although I am the first to admit that it isn't easy. But He does the helping if we only let Him.

Simon and I certainly learnt a great deal about nursing during those few weeks and also how versatile the nurses and doctors have to be. Sarah's drips were sometimes so complicated and really needed expert plumbing skills to fit them all up correctly. The kindness, dedication and efficiency of the staff had impressed us from the very start and this efficiency was demonstrated most clearly by Sister when Sarah's drip leaked whilst she was being given some blood and had to be repaired. We also learnt a great deal about leukaemia. Prior to Sarah's illness, we didn't really know much about it and assumed that it is always fatal, which is not so.

We discovered (to give a simple layman's explanation) that blood consists of a fluid part, called plasma, and non-fluid parts called cells. The cells are made in the bone marrow, and are then carried round the body to do their different jobs. There are three types of cells: red cells, which carry oxygen round the body, white cells which attack infection in the body and lastly platelets, which help blood to clot and controls bleeding. In a leukaemic patient there are other, non-functional, immature white cells also being made in the bone marrow. These 'blast cells' circulate in the blood stream and displace the good cells until, if left untreated, they simply take over. So the child with leukaemia may have reduced red cells, giving rise to anaemia; few white cells, so he cannot fight infection; and reduced platelets, which can obviously cause bleeding. In Sarah's case, she had nose-bleeds and also tiny purpura and bruises—all bleeding under the surface.

Left untreated, leukaemia is rapidly fatal, but in the last ten years enormous progress has been achieved in treating the disease and now 50 per cent of children who have been treated will be alive and well five years after completing a two or three year course of treatment.

There are two different types of leukaemia—myloid and lymphoblastic. Again, there are two different sorts of lymphoblastic and Sarah had acute lymphoblastic, which can be further divided into four more types. Sarah's, unfortunately, was not as treatable as other types, but we did not know this at the time and I'm extremely glad that we didn't. At the beginning it was enough for us to cope with the knowledge that she had a potentially fatal disease.

The basic treatment for leukaemia consists of a combination of chemotherapy (which consists of drugs given sometimes by injection, sometimes intravenously and also taken in tablet form) and radiotherapy, which eradicates the leukaemic cells or prevents them entering the spinal fluid and the brain. Lumbar punctures, which are injections into the spinal cord, are also given for this reason. Obviously, as the cells are formed in the bone marrow, bone marrow tests, requiring a general anaesthetic, are sometimes necessary when a more accurate analysis of the bone marrow and cell formation is required.

The initial period of treatment is called the induction period and at the end of this time (in Sarah's case about six to seven weeks) the leukaemic cells have all been knocked out of the body and the patient is said to be 'in remission'. Then follows maintenance treatment which involves more chemotherapy, regular hospital check-ups and blood counts and a generally careful watch on the child. However, by this stage the child can lead as normal a life as possible and can usually return to school.

All the drugs can have side effects. They are obviously extremely powerful—they have to be. Fortunately, Sarah's side effects were minimal, although she hated taking her steroid tablets which not only made her starving hungry, but also made her irritable, which she herself was aware of. As a result of the radiation treatment, her pretty blonde hair all fell out until she was completely bald, but she soon accepted this and we became quite used to her wearing one of several hats we bought her. Not only did this hide her baldness, but it also kept her warmer. Very often children wear wigs but Sarah was happier with her hats.

The hospital staff were all absolutely wonderful. We were extremely lucky to be living within half an hour from a hospital where they treat leukaemia. In fact there were at this time only about a dozen leukaemia units in the whole of England.

This particular leukaemia unit had only been in operation for about five years, and before that a leukaemia patient in our area would have had to travel much farther afield. Living so close to the hospital was marvellous for us and meant that there was not as much strain on our family as there would have been if we had had to do a lot of travelling.

The staff were concerned not just with the child but with the whole family. They were also not just concerned with treating the disease itself, but with helping the child and the rest of the family to come to terms with the illness and accept it and try to live as normal and as full a life as possible.

We got to know the staff quite well and there was no change of personnel, which was good for the stability and security of the patients and their parents. They were all quite used to the worries and fears experienced by families, and the problems that were quite normal results of the pressure and strain of coping with such a serious disease. What surprised us most was that they were so warm and caring. I would have thought that dealing with a disease like leukaemia, and especially among children, one would have to become slightly detached in order to do one's job properly. But they weren't. They were an amazing mixture of expert medical skill, total dedication and warm caring personality. They were all wonderful with the children, full of jokes and fun. We found out later that one of the team was the mother of a child who had died from a form of cancer and we were most impressed by her cheerfulness and complete dedication to people who were going through exactly what she herself must have experienced.

I suppose the leukaemia unit could best be described as a sort of extended family, everyone getting to know everyone else and everyone helping one another. Other parents too, were a tremendous source of help and encouragement. When Sarah was first admitted I met two mothers whose children had both been having treatment for over two years and they were so kind and understanding. I had a good cry and a chat and a cup of tea with them in the parents' waiting room and they helped me so much. Just meeting and chatting to other parents and finding out that they had experienced the same worries and heartaches, the same awful shock, but had managed to cope, was very comforting. So too was the fact that so many children were doing so well after a considerable length of time on treatment.

Sarah's treatment these first few days was extremely critical, as her leukaemia count, that is the number of leukaemia cells in her blood stream, was very high indeed. She remained on a drip and was given intravenous injections round the clock. She was also put on a fairly high dose of steroids. Her drugs were extremely powerful, in fact adults apparently would not be able to tolerate such a high dosage without being knocked flat and having complications with their liver, but children can and do cope with such high drug dosages. Sarah was no exception and, although she was very ill and feeling the effects of so many drugs, she remained remarkably cheerful and seemed to accept her illness.

6: Home again

Since Tuesday, when Sarah had first been admitted, I had had very little sleep and by Friday I was nearly exhausted both physically and emotionally, and very near to tears. So Simon suggested that I should go home for the weekend. I didn't want to leave Sarah, but knew that I had to get some sleep and also that, for the other children's sakes, it would be good for me to be at home with them for a while. So, reluctantly, I went home for three nights, coming back to the hospital in the daytime for brief visits to relieve Simon.

On Sunday morning I took the children to Mass early, at 8.15. I was looking forward to seeing our parish priest, Father Cashin, and asking for his prayers. My heart sank when I discovered that there was another, unfamiliar priest in his place, and then, even worse, to discover that Father Cashin was in fact away. In my greatest hour of need, even my parish priest wasn't there. I felt very lonely, but now I believe that God in His goodness allowed Father Cashin to be away, so that I would turn to Him—which is in fact what I did.

Originally Dr Davidson had told us to expect Sarah to be in hospital for at least a month—possibly even six weeks, so after the weekend Simon and I took turns staying the night at the hospital, so that one of us would always be with Sarah, and the children would see both of us too. It worked very well indeed. Usually I stayed at the hospital all day, but Simon came in for long stretches too.

All this time the strain was really hard and one of the worst things was not being able to talk to each other, so every chance to have five minutes together was precious. One day we managed to walk out of the hospital together. We walked past a church that I hadn't even noticed before and saw that it was a Catholic church. I suggested to Simon that we went in and said a prayer, and he readily agreed. This was the first of many occasions when we actually prayed together, and for both of us, this was one of the turning points in our lives. We were realising that we couldn't manage on our own, and together we started to reach out to God. It was this reaching out together that brought us closer to each other and, in due course, closer to God.

Because of her treatment, Sarah's resistance to infection was lowered and there was the constant risk of infection. She was therefore in a room of her own and also on what is called 'barrier nursing'. This meant that everyone entering her room had to don masks and gowns, to prevent any possible risk of Sarah picking up an infection from them. This rule did not apply to her immediate family, however, as the doctors sensibly explained to us that Sarah was going to have to get used to our germs. We did, however, make sure that we washed our hands well with the powerful hand disinfectant solution that all the hospital staff used.

That first week Sarah had several callers, including her class teacher and headmistress from school, who waved to her from the window. She also had masses of cards, letters and presents. Her room was soon full to bursting with cards taped to every available surface. She was especially fond of the homemade cards that every child in her school made her. Most of her visitors only waved through the window, but four special visitors were allowed in to see her—her dear friend Clara, her sister Alexandra and their parents Tim and Maria. Maria and the girls were soon flying to Paraguay since Tim and Maria had decided to separate. We were all terribly sad but fortunately, when they came in, Sarah didn't realise it would be the last time that she would ever see them. She was just delighted to see them, especially as they were allowed into her room, and she joked with them about how funny they looked with their masks on.

Sarah's treatment continued and the signs were very encouraging. Her appetite started coming back a bit—she was on a very high dose of prednisone, a steroid drug which had the side effect of making her ravenously hungry, and also seemed to give her food 'fads'. She started fancying cold sausages and Simon would cook at least a pound of them at home and bring them in to the hospital with him. Sarah would eat them all and then ask for more! It was good to see her eating again, she was so painfully thin when she was admitted.

The Wednesday after that first weekend, I had stayed the night at home, it being Simon's turn to spend the night at the hospital. Every other Wednesday in Ross Catholic church there is a school Mass which usually only the Catholic children attend. This particular Wednesday, however, the Mass was to be offered specially for Sarah and the whole school was invited to attend if they wished. The school was closed for the first part of the morning to enable all the teachers to go to the Mass.

I went to the Mass with Stephen, who had just broken up for his summer holidays, Rebecca and Hannah, and Hugues, our French boy, who also expressed the desire to come with us.

It was a most moving experience for all present. The church was packed to bursting. Jenny, and some of Sarah's closest friends at school, did the readings and bidding prayers (specially written prayers offered for particular needs). The songs were simple and beautiful. Prayers were offered up for Sarah, her twin sister Jenny, and all their family. I felt overwhelmed by the strength, visible and inward, of everyone's prayers and feelings for us all. This was the first of many times that I sensed, without doubt, the wonderful power of prayer and it filled me with such strength and gratitude. I could feel deep within me a great sense of strength and love that was coming as a direct response from everyone's prayers for us. And although I was concerned about Sarah and her illness, I knew a marvellous feeling of peace and, in a strange sense, of joy too that was stronger than anything I had ever felt before, and which was deeper and more powerful than even my concern and my anguish.

After the Mass, during which many of the parents in particular had been moved to tears, one friend asked me how it was that I had managed to stay dry-eyed, and I wondered myself. But I know that God was giving us strength and therefore I knew I had to try hard to trust Him. Even Hugues found the service that morning very moving and edifying. I was only sorry that Simon could not have been there with me, but he was with Sarah.

Our prayers were answered. Sarah responded very well indeed to the treatment. We were delighted, and concentrated our efforts on making her comfortable, reading to her and playing games to stop her being bored and to help her not to be too homesick, which she was continually.

Sarah was doing so well that Dr Davidson decided that she could come home after a fortnight. Her treatment would still be continuing and every few days she would have to go back into the hospital for injections, but otherwise she would now be on tablets several times a day. We were all so excited about her coming home, particularly Sarah herself. We packed up all her bits and pieces, said our thanks and goodbyes, collected bottles of tablets, and drove her home. She was obviously very weak still, but so excited to be going home, and Simon and I were really happy at the thought of having our family together again. The strain of the last two weeks had been felt by us all, but we were so lucky compared to lots of families. We were within twenty minutes drive of the hospital so we were able to go in frequently and were near enough for Simon or me to stay the night. Also, we were in the fortunate position of Simon being self-employed, so he could take time off work. At that particular time we were also lucky in having Hugues, who had originally come to gain some farm experience and to learn a bit of English, but was indispensible when Simon needed to be in the hospital. It meant there was another pair of hands to milk the cow, feed the pigs, or pick produce for market.

Sarah's white cell count was still very low, which meant that she was wide open to infection, and we were advised not to have friends in but just to let her get used to family germs. We also went home armed with bottles of the powerful hand disinfectant solution which we had used in the hospital for everyone to wash their hands with on entering the house, especially when coming in from the farm.

Sarah had to return to the hospital every few days for injections and also for more lumbar punctures, which she hated as she didn't like having a general anaesthetic. Firstly, being on prednisone she was always hungry and having to starve in the morning was sheer agony. Secondly, she hated the actual sensation of 'going to sleep'. Those Wednesdays were some of our worst in the hospital and I would gladly have had the anaesthetic myself; it hurt so much watching her go through her ordeal. I would have to fight back my tears, often unsuccessfully, as I went out of the treatment room after she had gone to sleep. I always stayed with her until then, praying silently, and then while she was having her lumbar puncture I would go out for a short walk around the block, have a cup of coffee and wait until she was ready to be carried back to her bed.

She was normally quite sleepy, as she wasn't sleeping well at nights, so the after effects of the anaesthetic was all she needed to send her into a much needed deep sleep. When she did wake up she was normally so hungry she implored me to ask for some food. Rather warily she was allowed a bit of toast and then more when she was obviously all right. She was only once sick after a lumbar puncture and then she was very sick for the whole day. I would bring her home as soon as possible, about lunchtime, tuck her up into her own bed, fix her a salad or whatever she fancied and then she would sleep or I would read to her.

We read some lovely books together. Simon would read her *Winnie the Pooh*, which he was brilliant at, and she adored listening to, for she had such a lovely sense of humour. I read several books to her including *Annie* and *Anne of Green Gables* (my own favourite). We had just started *The Little Prince* a few days before she died.

At the same time as her lumbar punctures were going on, Sarah started radiation treatment. Simon and I both took her over, with Hannah and Rebecca, for the initial appointment, when the treatment was explained to us and Sarah was shown the huge machines. It was a very friendly, light, airy place with hundreds of pot plants. Sarah lay as still as could be on a huge table which went up and down and tilted in each direction at the press of a button. Various pictures were taken and a mask made for her. This involved putting a sort of muslin on her face and some warm plastic-type material on top which moulded to the shape of her face. Sarah was patient and unflinching as ever while the technicians very carefully moulded the mask on her face.

The day of Sarah's first treatment we went to Cheltenham as usual but this time to another room with a similar machine, absolutely huge. Sarah lay down and the girls fitted her mask on and adjusted the table she was lying on, and so on. Then we all had to leave. I hated this—and I also hated seeing the little red light glowing, showing that radiation was in process. We could see Sarah lying so still, like something out of a science fiction movie, but I couldn't watch while the radiation was in progress. I prayed. Half a minute, then they went in and turned the machine over, then another half a minute. It was all over so quickly, it was actually a bit of an anticlimax, but Sarah was wonderfully cheerful and we drove home, planning what we would do and eat that day.

Simon and I took it in turns to drive Sarah to Cheltenham and in all she made ten trips for treatment. The two worst days were Wednesdays when she had to go from Cheltenham on to Gloucester for lumbar puctures. We were all pleased when the radiation treatment was over, as we could try to return to a more normal pattern of life, and Sarah would soon be on 'maintenance', which meant that her body had now rid itself of all the leukaemic cells in her blood. Now it was just a question of keeping them away so she would have new drugs, some to take daily, some once a week and others to take daily for a period of a week.

Remembering her tablets was something of a nightmare; to start with there were so many different tablets, and she had to take some twice a day, others once a day. I tried to have a strict routine about giving her the tablets, and would double check the bottles each time for fear of giving her the wrong tablet by accident. I must say Sarah was fantastic, swallowing sometimes as many as twenty tablets a day with no more than the occasional complaint. She taught us so much in that period: acceptance, patience, trust, love and hope. We have learnt so very much from her and continue to even now.

She was so cheerful, in spite of often feeling ill, in spite of all her treatment, and through her illness she became even more loving. In her own brokenness, Sarah was becoming very close to Christ and He was very quietly and very beautifully working through her.

7: Our island holiday

Sarah's response to her treatment was very encouraging indeed. She really sailed through this first induction period and suffered no ill-effects at all from the radiation treatment. She was to suffer loss of her hair and a feeling of intense tiredness later, but at this time she was really feeling much stronger and fitter.

Two things then happened. Firstly, Sarah was put on maintenance drugs which were intended to be her mainstay for the next two or three years. This meant that the lumbar punctures and radiation were finished, and her only treatment now was her various tablets. We welcomed this change of treatment as it gave us hope and enabled Sarah to return to what we hoped would be a more normal way of life: going out, meeting friends, even going back to school.

Her education was now in the hands of a Mrs Lowe, who had been allocated to her as a home tutor. Sarah and Mrs Lowe soon became great friends and Sarah very much enjoyed the companionship and the stimulus of work. Mrs Lowe was careful not to overtire her so they did a fair amount of art and craft which Sarah loved. We were very fortunate indeed to have such a kind and understanding woman as Sarah's home tutor and although I sometimes wished that I could devote as much time to Sarah on my own, I was nevertheless grateful to have time to give to the others and to be able to get back to a more normal pattern of life myself.

All during Sarah's stay in hospital, from the time when her leukaemia had first been diagnosed, our friends had been fantastic. As well as flowers and presents, letters and cards, we received offers of help both with the children and with the farm. We were extremely touched and also very grateful for all the offers of help and with the school holidays just starting, it was good for the children to be able to go and play with friends.

I have mentioned Russell and Anne, the parents of Rebecca's closest friend, James. Anne soon became Hannah's second mother and used to look after her whenever I needed to go to the hospital with Sarah. Hannah loved Anne and became very used to being dropped off at her house. James and his two elder brothers were very good with Hannah and it was marvellous for me to be able to leave Hannah with them all, often at very short notice, and know that she was so happy. I shall never be able to thank Anne enough for all she did for us.

Mondays were hospital days. Anne would normally have Rebecca and Hannah but I did take them to the hospital sometimes. This wasn't easy, particularly if we had a long wait, but it was a source of distraction for Sarah to have them with her. Those Mondays consisted of having a blood test, then a wait while the results were being analysed, then in to see either Dr Davidson or Dr Murray, who, on the basis of the blood count and a thorough examination, would recommend the dosage of tablets for the forthcoming week. Then there was another wait at the dispensary for the tablets, sometimes as much as an hour. In all, having left home shortly before 9 a.m., we were rarely back by lunchtime, but Sarah was always so patient and uncomplaining.

On the practical side I was finding it increasingly difficult to manage running the house. We had tried desperately hard to find a mother's help, but found it impossible to find the right person. There again, looking back on it, God was so good not letting us find one. Those last few months were so precious to our family life, we wouldn't have wanted an outsider with us then. Instead, we were given a home help, from the county council, who was very kind and the most fantastic worker. Shirly just walked into the house and whizzed through everything with such thoroughness that it left us all amazed. We all started to be tidier simply because if we left anything on the floor Shirley would pick it up and wash and iron it before we knew it!

On Mondays I could just leave everything, beds unmade, dirty dishes in the kitchen and we would return at lunchtime to a perfectly tidy, much cleaner house. This was a marvellous help to me, for I should never have managed on my own. Shirley had herself lost a child, not from illness, but in a tragic accident in a fire. When Sarah died we were both, I think, able to help each other, and certainly we had a deep common bond between us.

The second major event at that time was that we went on holiday. By the beginning of September when Sarah started on maintenance, we were all feeling in great need of a holiday. We don't normally ever go on holiday at all and apart from staying with our parents and also with my brother in France, we had never really taken a 'family holiday'. In the summer we were always too busy, and it is difficult to leave the market garden and animals at any time of the year. Then there was also the question of Sarah's health and the fact that if she picked up an infection or developed a temperature, she would have to go to hospital right away.

For some time, we had all been longing to go and stay on the tiny island of Herm, just off Guernsey in the Channel Islands. One of my brothers, Peter, with his wife Martine and their three children, were living there. Peter was working on the island farm and Martine was starting up her own pottery there.

We had heard so much about this tiny island (just one and a half miles long by half a mile wide), its lovely beaches and beautiful scenery; the fact that it was reached by ferry from Guernsey; that it only had one pub, one hotel and no cars. We all thought it sounded perfect and just the place for us to go to get away from the pressures of the past eight weeks.

We talked it over with the doctors and they were in complete agreement. We were delighted! Dr Davidson said reassuringly that Sarah could always be taken to hospital by RAF helicopter if an emergency arose! We prayed that one wouldn't and in fact we didn't worry about that possibility at all. We were all just so excited and had great fun planning and packing. For Jenny and Stephen there was an added bonus, for it meant that they were also missing a week of school. Little were we all to know just how precious this week was to be for us.

We had decided to fly, for although vastly more expensive, we could fly to Guernsey direct from Gloucester. This would be far less tiring for Sarah and more important, it also carried less risk of infection for her than on a longer ferry journey.

Our holiday was perfect. The flights there and back were as smooth as could be and even I enjoyed them, although my dislike of flying is a family joke. The first two nights we stayed at a family hotel in Guernsey, which was great fun. We were within a short walk of a sheltered beach and we also went into the town and explored the local shops.

We had all been anticipating with great delight the short ferry journey to Herm and a very excited family boarded the ferry for the twenty-minute sea journey. My brother had met us at the airport when we had arrived in Guernsey and stayed with us for a while before returning to Herm. Now, on arrival in Herm, we were greeted by his wife, Martine and their three children. It was lovely to see them all again and fantastic to have arrived on the island.

Herm was absolutely beautiful and just right for us at that time. It was so peaceful, and my brother had arranged for us to have a flat, with lots of room and very well furnished, just two minutes from a lovely beach. We had a very relaxed five days. We went to the beach, explored a little (Sarah became remarkably stronger while we were there and managed to walk far more than we had expected), picked blackberries, of which there were hundreds, visited Peter and Martine, played with their children. It was such a fun time and so good to be together. We all needed this period just to be together and, grateful as we were to the hospitals and doctors and nurses, it was fantastic not to have to think about going to the hospital for one whole week! We all thoroughly relaxed and the sea air helped us all to sleep well too. Even Hannah slept really soundly.

The island itself, although tiny, was not flat as we had expected but quite hilly in places. There were lots of beautiful beaches, all very different. One day we went to Shell Beach, which is so named because it is made up of thousands of tiny shells. It was so warm that day that everyone went swimming; then we collected lots of the different little shells. We had the whole long beach to ourselves and it was just beautiful.

The beach nearest to our flat was very sheltered, in a sort of cove. The sand was almost white and the children had great fun building sandcastles or drawing on the sand. We were very fortunate that the weather wasn't really hot as for Sarah there was little shade on the beaches, but it was warm enough to play on the beach and although the sea seemed icy cold, Jenny went swimming and the little ones paddled.

We cooked very simple meals in our flat. We had ordered all our groceries in advance as they had to come over from Guernsey on the ferry but you could buy butter, bread and, of course, milk on the island.

We visited the farm and were amazed to think that even the cows had to go to market on the ferry. And of course the milk was taken down to the ferry each day. In the summer when the island is visited by literally thousands of holidaymakers each day, ferries run frequently to and from the mainland, but in the winter there are only two ferries a day. Very occasionally the ferries don't operate because the weather is too bad.

It seemed very strange for us to go shopping by boat. Quite an adventure in fact. At home in Gloucestershire, I don't really think twice about getting in the car to go into our nearest town, four miles away, to go shopping and if I have forgotten something that I am desperate for I can, at least, get in the car and go and get it. Not so on Herm. If you were making a cake and suddenly realised you had no flour (as I have been known to do), you would just have to go without, or borrow some from a neighbour.

And when you do go shopping, at least in the wintertime, you go over to Guernsey on the early morning ferry and have to wait till the late afternoon before you can get back to Herm. And of course, there is always the chance that having left to go shopping in the morning, the weather might turn too stormy for the ferry even to run at all to get you back in the afternoon!

A week passed very quickly and all too soon it was time to pack our suitcases, say our farewells and catch the ferry back to Guernsey. The weather was very stormy that night and the sea had actually been extremely rough for most of the week. I lay in bed listening to the wind howling the night before we left and prayed so hard for a smooth crossing; having all the children thrown about and feeling seasick would be such a sad end to our lovely holiday. In answer to my prayers, on the morning of our departure there were blue skies and radiant sunshine. We had a perfect crossing and an even more perfect flight, with spectacular views the entire way back. As we only flew at 9,000 feet, and there were no clouds at all, it was just like flying over a giant map of England and certainly much better than any geography lesson!

I felt so grateful to God for our lovely holiday and for keeping Sarah well and for our peaceful journey home. We returned home feeling really refreshed and relaxed. However, the benefits of our holiday were yet to be fully known. How even more grateful we were to be for that week together, after Sarah died, and how much more were we to treasure the memories of such a happy family holiday.

8: In thee, oh Lord, I put my trust

Life returned to normal again. Stephen and Jenny went back to school and Sarah resumed her lessons with her home tutor. We had been expecting Sarah to feel tired as a result of her radiation treatment and sure enough she did start feeling very tired about six weeks after the treatment, which is normally the case. She had very long rests in the daytime, but we were not concerned, as we had been forewarned to expect this sort of reaction. Apart from the tiredness she was feeling extremely well.

We started living much more normally again; in fact, if Sarah hadn't have felt so tired, we might have considered sending her back to school. Another reason not to was that there was chickenpox in her class—one of the dreaded diseases for leukaemics—so she continued to stay at home. She was so happy and was getting on with her home tutor so well, that this seemed ideal.

We went to the eye hospital for her six-monthly check up and she was doing so well that they said she would soon only need to go to an optician to check her glasses. We were thrilled; Sarah had undergone three eye operations for a squint in the past five years, and the last one really seemed to have done the trick.

On Wednesday, 13 October, I had attended a healing service in our own Catholic church. It was a service held monthly and organised by the various different churches in the town. I had never been to a healing service before and I don't know what prompted me to go to this one; I just felt in some way drawn to go. Jenny volunteered to come with me.

The first part of the service consisted of different people sharing readings and prayers. We sang some hymns and also had a short sermon about healing given by one of the ministers. Then I saw that people were going up to the front of the church and two people were laying their hands on them and praying for them.

I wasn't sure whether I could go up to have them pray for us and never really intended to go up to the front. But I did, and when it was my turn found myself in front of Father Cashin and another man I didn't know. I said that I wanted to thank God for helping us all so much since Sarah had become ill and to ask Him to carry on helping us. Father Cashin explained to the other man about Sarah and her leukaemia and they then, very gently but firmly, placed their hands on my head and on my shoulders and started praying. I don't remember what they said but while they were praying I suddenly felt a most powerful feeling run right through me. The only way that I can describe it is that it was just like an electric shock, very sudden, extremely powerful, actually warm but not in the least painful.

When they had finished their prayers, I returned to my seat and felt completely peaceful. I knew now that God was in control of the situation and that He would help us. And He most definitely was in control of the situation, but we were not to realise exactly to what extent until much later on.

On the Friday night, two days later, we had been invited out to supper with some friends and, rather than get a babysitter, we took the children with us, as Sarah was feeling really well. We were all so delighted with her progress and felt very confident of the future. It never entered our minds that the treatment wouldn't carry on as it was.

On Sunday, Sarah had her normal after-lunch sleep in her room. I went up to see her at about four and I could see straight away from her flushed face that she had a temperature. I felt her cheeks—they were very hot, and taking her temperature confirmed my suspicions. All during her treatment we had been told to be watchful for a temperature and we knew we should notify the hospital immediately. We had, up till now, been extremely lucky. We knew from other parents that leukaemics tend to get temperatures very easily, sometimes frequently, and as they couldn't control the fever themselves needed to be put on a drip, which meant of course, going into hospital. We were not unduly concerned about Sarah's temperature but rang Dr Davidson who suggested we wait for a bit and give him another ring at six o'clock to let him know how it was. It was still the same at six and so he said he was very sorry but she really ought to be brought in. Sarah was rather upset about this but I told her it probably wouldn't be for long and I would stay with her all the time and Daddy would come and spend the night.

I drove her into Gloucester where she was examined. They found nothing at all to explain her temperature but took a routine blood test. Sarah and I waited patiently for the results, anticipating that we could then both return home. However, when Dr Davidson came in I could see he was distressed. He said that he was very sorry but he didn't like the look of some of her cells, so they would have to do a bone marrow test in the morning. I was quite stunned; it had come out of the blue, when she was doing so well. My saddest thoughts were for Sarah, who hated the idea of having another drip and, worse still, a general anaesthetic. I promised I would be with her all the time.

Simon spent the night with her at the hospital as he'd promised and I took over from him early the next morning in time for the bone marrow test. Sarah wasn't very happy but fortunately she didn't have to wait too long before they came to fetch her. I carried her into the theatre and stood by her as she was put to sleep.

While she was having her bone marrow test I tried not to cry and prayed so hard: 'Please God, let it be all right and give us the strength to cope and trust you.'

Later, Simon reappeared and Sarah came round after her anaesthetic, but then went back to sleep again. We waited together, quietly, anxiously, for the results of the test.

Dr Davidson was completely honest, as always, which we both respected and were grateful for. The news, he said, was not good. Sarah's bone marrow test showed that leukaemic cells were evident again in the marrow itself, so her treatment would have to be changed as the present one was no longer effective. It meant that she would be put on what they called CHOP, involving a day's or night's treatment with drugs being given intravenously, by drip, every three weeks. However, it was unlikely that even CHOP would be effective for too long. She would perhaps at the most have a year, but possibly only months before she relapsed again.

We inwardly choked back the tears. The position had become so different. Sarah would now be lucky to have a year to live; it seemed difficult to believe or imagine. Dr Davidson went on to explain how important our role would be in making the rest of her life as happy as possible. We both realised we had been given a tremendously difficult task, but in a way we were lucky. Yes, we knew now that Sarah would almost certainly die but we also knew that it was up to us, and us alone—with God's help—to make her life as happy as possible.

At least Sarah was still alive and in a way, as long as someone is still alive there is still hope. Death still seems too unreal for us to grasp that it will happen. But we were simply grateful that we did have advance warning that she would die, rather than have it happen suddenly, and we did also have this wonderful chance of being able to try to make the rest of Sarah's life as happy for her as we could.

We also realised how important it would be for all our family that these last months together were as happy as we could make them. This doesn't mean that we decided to do anything different from our normal pattern of life. On the contrary, we tried to lead as normal a life as possible, but also as happy a life as possible.

That evening, Simon and I went for a short walk together while a nurse kept Sarah company. We needed a little time on our own. We both cried and prayed and comforted each other. We passed a Catholic church where we had been before to pray. 'Let's go in,' I suggested. We entered, the church was quite quiet and empty. We both prayed for strength and courage to do what was right. We felt slightly better, but our hearts ached.

On the way back to the hospital we talked about whether or

not we should tell anyone of Sarah's relapse and what it meant. We both decided not to do anything for the moment, but to think about it. We had only just managed to make our family and friends feel easier about accepting that Sarah had a possibly fatal disease. We had tried so hard to allay their doubts and fears and now they were all much happier about it. There *is* so much that can be done with children suffering from leukaemia, and the prognosis is so much better now than it was ten years ago. If we told them that Sarah would probably now die, it would cast such a black cloud on everyone's lives, and put them all under a great deal of unnecessary strain. Also, Sarah's life would not be normal as people would be bound to treat her differently if they knew. So we decided not to tell anyone yet, except for two people. One was Stephen's headmaster at school; the other our parish priest. With Stephen a weekly boarder, we felt it only fair to let his headmaster know the exact position in case we should at any time want Stephen home in a hurry, and also as he was acting as guardian for Stephen. We also told Father Cashin, who was very kind and definitely agreed with us that Sarah shouldn't know. After all, he pointed out, miracles do happen and it would be dreadful to tell her and then for her to worry unnecessarily. However, we were equally of the opinion that we must be completely honest with her and would certainly answer any questions truthfully when and if they arose.

That Monday, Sarah was given the same drugs through a drip that she had had in July, to get her into remission. The next stage was to give her the CHOP treatment, and this would happen on Tuesday which, as it happened, was my birthday. Birthdays are always great fun in our house and even Simon and I have to have a proper 'party tea', as the children call it. We had explained to Sarah that they were going to change her treatment and, instead of having to take so many tablets each day, she was now going to have CHOP, which meant having to come in once every three or four weeks to have some medicine through a drip. She welcomed the idea of taking fewer tablets, but the only drawback about CHOP was that it tends to make children feel very sick so they are given a sedative to help reduce this.

Sarah was disappointed to be staying in hospital for my birthday but I cheerfully told her that that didn't matter, we'd all come in and have our birthday tea in her room. This cheered her up considerably and we made lists of food for the party.

On my birthday morning I made a cake very early, having been too tired to do so the night before, after I returned home from the hospital. Amazingly, it turned out beautifully even though I had made it on the kitchen table at the same time as getting the breakfast! I wanted to be at the hospital early, and fortunately my mother had come to stay, on hearing Sarah was in hospital again. She promised to bring the children and the cooled, iced cake in later. It was a birthday I shall never forget.

On arriving at the hospital everyone wished me a happy birthday. Sarah was thrilled to see me, though very fed up with being in hospital and obviously not feeling well. There were lots of cards for me to open including one from the ward staff, and people popped in and out all morning, wishing me a happy birthday. It was a happy day, in spite of the fact that Simon and I knew this would possibly be the last birthday of mine that we would have with Sarah—but then, weren't we lucky having her for this one! Increasingly, from now onwards, we counted each day of having Sarah as an extra blessing.

Dr Murray came in and wanted to see me. She wondered if, as the family were all coming in, they could possibly do blood tests on us all. This was to see if there was any chance that one of us matched Sarah well enough to be a donor for a bone marrow transplant for her. We had known that they would eventually do these tests but Dr Murray wondered if we could do them today. In view of the fact that it was my birthday she didn't want to spoil the day, but if all the family would be there it would save us all trooping in another day and it would also be good to find out as soon as possible if Sarah could have a bone marrow transplant. I said that of course it would be perfectly all right to do the blood tests today but we would need to get Stephen over from school, so

I rang the school and they arranged to bring Stephen over to meet Simon on the way to Gloucester. How kind God was being to us. He knew this would be one of our last few family birthday parties together, so how lovely to have Stephen there too, and all be together.

We all had our blood taken (it made a change for Sarah for *us* to have the injections) and afterwards we had our tea party. I had been out to buy goodies for the party, so we had crisps and other savoury biscuits, sandwiches, which Granny had made, coke and lemonade, birthday cake and wine. We gave all the staff a piece of cake and a glass of wine and they were most appreciative.

Tea over, the family left, except for me. I stayed to be with Sarah and Simon went home to see to the animals but to return later. The drugs for CHOP arrived and were given to Sarah, together with Phenergan, to reduce the feeling of nausea. The house doctor sat on Sarah's bed with me. The Phenergan seemed to be having no effect so Sarah was given more and then she started pounding her fists and having what looked to me to be a sort of fit. If the doctor hadn't been so self-composed I would have been extremely worried; as it was, it was a frightening experience to see Sarah in such a state. Eventually she was given Valium which put her to sleep. It was then realised that the Phenergan had given her this very bad reaction—most uncommon and very unfortunate. I was so utterly relieved when Sarah did fall asleep, and when Simon arrived she was sleeping peacefully. However, that night, because she obviously couldn't be given any more Phenergan, she felt extremely nauseous and Simon spent most of the night up with her as she was sick again and again.

It seemed so awful that Sarah had to go through such a dreadful time and it hurt us both deeply to watch. The next morning she was feeling very weak but remembered nothing of the previous night's reactions to Phenergan, only the sickness. She was allowed to come home after a couple of days, for which we were grateful, and of course she was delighted to be home, and soon started to feel much stronger.

The results of the family's blood tests came through two days after my birthday. It was a nerve-wracking experience.

Dr Murray had invited me to sit in the office with her while she telephoned Bristol to get the results of the tests. Strangely enough, when she told me the results—that there was no hope of a bone marrow transplant—I was more relieved than disappointed. Of course it was disappointing that Sarah couldn't have a transplant, but a great relief that she wouldn't have to go through another ordeal, and one which offered no 100 per cent chance of success, but would mean going to a strange hospital and being away from home for some time. I was relieved that Sarah would be able to stay with us and be at home, though of course now we knew for certain that her treatment would not be able to keep her alive indefinitely.

Ironically enough, Stephen and Jenny's blood had matched perfectly on all seven counts.

Simon and I discussed again the question of telling anyone about Sarah's relapse, but we were both in total agreement that it should be our secret. We found hidden strength to cope with this latest development, and tried not to think of the future but to concentrate on each day at a time.

9: May the Lord raise you up

About ten days after CHOP, the treatment is expected to have knocked out all leukaemic cells but in doing so, as with all treatment for leukaemia, the drugs also unfortunately knock out a lot of other important cells, particularly white cells. So the child becomes very susceptible to infection, having little resistance. Sarah's particular dosage of CHOP (there are various strengths) was extremely strong and so about ten days afterwards she was very susceptible to infections of any sort. We had been warned of this and told not to worry if she produced a temperature round about that time. Some children, we were reassured, produced a fever as regular as clockwork when they are on CHOP, and were in and out of hospital every ten days or so.

On the Sunday when Sarah had reached this stage of her treatment, my two youngest brothers came and spent the day with us. We had a great time; the children adore their uncles and always enjoy their visits. They all played cricket after lunch Sarah joining in the fun as much as anyone else. That evening after they had left, Sarah produced a temperature, which was still there an hour later, so I rang Dr Murray, who said that Sarah should go in. So a very sad Sarah was driven to Gloucester by her Daddy. She felt so well and had had such a super day. We all consoled ourselves with the fact that we had had a happy day together and at least Sarah's temperature hadn't come on earlier. I stayed at home with the others and left the children with Anne the next morning, so I could relieve Simon and go into the hospital.

They found nothing to explain Sarah's temperature and after a thorough examination, and having got her temperature down a bit, decided to let her come home. We were thrilled! They did take a throat swab and also a swab of a tiny pimple on her arm, but we thought nothing more about either and went home again.

The next morning, however, I had a phone call from Dr Murray, saying that the swab test on the spot on Sarah's arm showed that she did have an infection, a particularly difficult one to treat any other way than intravenously. So she was very sorry, but could we please bring Sarah back in right away. Sarah's arm was actually quite sore by now and her spot had got visibly larger, so when we had arrived at the hospital I was quite relieved that they were going to treat it.

She was put on a drip and given new drugs to combat the infection, which was called pseudomonas and was extremely dangerous—mainly affecting premature babies and people like leukaemics whose resistance to infection is low. Also, ironically enough, it is probably picked up in hospitals. Sarah didn't show much improvement, and the next day Dr Murray talked to Simon and me.

'I'm afraid,' she said, 'the infection Sarah has is very serious indeed. I feel it's only fair to tell you that it really is very serious.'

'You mean, it could kill her?'

'Yes, I'm afraid so,' she replied. 'We shall try giving her these drugs and if these don't work we may give her some extra white cells. I've alerted them in Bristol already, just in case.'

At this point I burst into tears. Dr Murray was very kind and after offering words of comfort left us alone together in the office. It was too soon. She couldn't die yet. Please God, don't let her die yet. 'We must be brave,' said Simon. I agreed, we had to be brave for Sarah and for the others.

Sarah's condition didn't get any better, in fact it became a lot worse, and what had been a tiny spot on her arm had soon extended to cover her entire forearm, and was extremely painful. She was hardly eating and not even sitting up any more. Simon and I took it in turns to read to her and talk to her and generally keep her company. The white cells were needed, it was decided, and they arrived by motorbike carrier on four consecutive days starting on Thursday. They were just like an ordinary drip really, though they posed some extraordinary plumbing feats for the nurses, as they had to be attached by means of a special pump. But Simon got the hang of it and was soon giving them advice on how to fit it all up!

Friday was Guy Fawkes night and each year they have fireworks for the children's ward. Sarah didn't miss out; she was carried by Simon, assisted by several nurses all holding onto different bits of her drip, into Sister's office where we all had a grandstand view of the fireworks. It was a superb display and I shall never forget that frail little body in her father's arms watching it.

Sarah didn't seem to be getting any better, even with the white cells. On Saturday I mentioned to her that Father Cashin had offered to bring her the Sacrament of the Sick and asked her if she would like him to come in. (She knew that this sacrament is given to people who are ill and nowadays sick people are given it readily, without there being any question of their dying.) She said she would like him to come in and he said that he would come on Sunday.

Sunday arrived, and all day Sarah asked when was Father Cashin coming. She was very, very weak and was speaking only in whispers. The doctor doing his rounds called in to see her in the afternoon and told me that all I could do now was pray. I knew and was praying more earnestly than ever before, 'Please, please don't let her die, not in the hospital, please, dear God.' Then Father Cashin arrived and gave Sarah the Sacrament of the Sick. This is a very simple and very beautiful sacrament which celebrates God's love and care for the whole person. God loves each one of us and wants us to have wholeness of life. But we are not whole, for all sorts of different reasons, and we need help to become whole. So God helps us by sharing His own life with us. This He does in all the sacraments, which are all an encounter, a meeting with Jesus Christ Himself. In this encounter, we are touched with God's own hands, He shares His own life, His own love with us and as a result of this, we are given inner strength and inner healing.

Through the Sacrament of the Sick, the sick person is given special strength and help from God to cope with his or her illness. The healing received sometimes does involve physical healing, and a person who has received this sacrament does sometimes get better. But the healing of the sacrament is much deeper than just physical healing, for it is the whole person that is involved. And the effects are very often noticed in the way in which the sick person is able to accept the illness, or is more peaceful and freed from worries and fears, and in the way in which his or her faith and trust in God is increased. For when we allow God in faith to touch us with His love, He does indeed do so.

The effects of the sacrament are not confined just to the sick person but very often to the whole family as well. When one member of a family is seriously ill, help is needed by the whole family to cope with the extra demands being made on it and God wants to help.

The sacrament itself is a short service, and consists of some very beautiful prayers, asking God to help the sick person and give newness of life in Him: 'Through this holy anointing may the Lord in His love and mercy help you with the grace of the Holy Spirit . . . May the Lord who frees you from sin save you and raise you up.'

Father Cashin very quietly and gently said these prayers. At the same time he anointed Sarah with oil on her forehead and on her hands. She was lying perfectly still, so very weak yet so very peaceful and seemed to have a total acceptance and trust in God.

Father Cashin then continued with more prayers, asking God to heal Sarah and give her His help:

Lord Jesus Christ
you chose to share our human nature
to redeem all people and to heal the sick.
Look with compassion upon your servant
whom we have anointed in your name with this holy oil
for the healing of her body and spirit.
Support her with your power,
comfort her with your protection,
and give her the strength to fight against evil.

Father Cashin, Simon and I then said the Lord's prayer together. After this, Father Cashin gave Sarah Holy Communion. She seemed so very close to God. We were all very moved by her complete acceptance of her illness and by the inner peace and joy that shone from within her, although she could barely speak or lift up her hands.

Finally Father Cashin gave Sarah a blessing with the following lovely words:

May God the Father bless you.
May God the Son heal you.
May God the Holy Spirit enlighten you.
May God protect you from harm and grant you salvation.
May He shine on your heart and lead you to eternal life. Amen

Simon and I were both very pleased that Father Cashin had come. And so was Sarah who did seem to be feeling a bit better.

I left late to go home, telling Simon to ring me if he needed me. I prayed all the way home and somehow I wasn't worried but knew that God was looking after us all. Deep inside me I knew Simon would ring and, sitting down to supper with my mother, who fortunately was again staying to help, I declined the glass of wine she offered me. Somehow I knew I needed to be in complete control of all my senses that night.

We were in the middle of supper when the phone rang. As soon as I heard Simon's voice I said, 'Do you need me?' 'Yes,' he replied. I didn't wait any longer, but slammed the receiver down and ran to get my coat. Running out of the house, I called to my startled mother, 'I'm needed at the hospital, call Anne to help you with Hannah,' and I was off.

It was dark and pouring with rain, I was shaking all over and I could hear my heart pounding as I drove. Well, actually I don't think I *did* drive; I think angels must have carried me along those slippery roads well in excess of sixty miles an hour. The entire way and the whole time I prayed over and over again, 'Please God, let me get there in time. Please don't let her die yet.' In particular I asked Our Lady for her help as I prayed the Hail Mary. Then, and for ever more, the final words of this beautiful prayer asking God's own mother to ask God to help us, became and will for me remain particularly meaningful:

Holy Mary, mother of God
pray for us sinners,
now and at the hour of our death. Amen

Of all people to ask for help, it seemed most natural for me to ask Mary to pray for me in my hour of need. Firstly, as a mother, she would so well understand how I felt. And, I instinctively turned to her, for Mary was so very special in that she so totally, so completely, and in such humility accepted God's will for her. Without her, there would have been no Jesus Christ. God could not have become man and for us that would have meant no salvation. We would not have been able to share in God's own life. So, not only was her role vital for us, she also gives us the most perfect example of how we, too, should allow God to work in us and through us.

So I asked Mary for her prayers, in accepting the will of God in my own life. And at that precise moment, I prayed with all my heart that this would not be the hour of Sarah's death, at least not before I arrived at the hospital.

To me it had seemed like an endless journey, but in fact I arrived at the hospital in a record fifteen minutes. I slammed the door of the car and ran up to the ward. It was very still and quiet. I caught my breath and gently opened the door to Sarah's room. The curtains were all drawn and she was lying in bed, so still and pale, breathing very lightly. Simon, who was at her side, turned round and smiled, surprised to see me so soon. 'I'm glad you've come,' he said. 'How is she?' I asked. Sarah, at this moment stirred. 'Mummy's here,' Simon told her and I went forward and kissed her. She smiled and squeezed my hand very gently. She looked so peaceful and happy and I was so grateful to be at her side with Simon. If she was going to die now, we would at least both be there with her. As she had just a few hours ago received both the Sacrament of the Sick and Holy Communion, she was also very close to God in a special way and completely at peace. And we too, felt this wonderful sense of deep peace.

Simon and I knelt by Sarah's side and prayed, and from time to time one of us dozed off on the put-up bed or in a chair. But God in His wisdom and love didn't let Sarah die that night. She battled on and both we and the nursing staff were surprised and delighted that she lasted through the night. The next morning Sarah actually looked better and sat up in bed, but she was still very weak. My mother brought Jenny and Stephen in to see her and she was as delighted to see them as they were to see her—particularly Stephen. He should really have been at school but under the circumstances, with Simon and me both in the hospital, it was difficult to take him back first thing and, more important, we wanted him to see Sarah.

Simon and I both stayed in the hospital for the next three days, Simon returning home for short spells in the daytime to see to the farm. But I could not face sleeping at home again with Sarah in the hospital. I knew I wouldn't sleep anyway and, camping next to Sarah, at least we were at her side and at this precise moment that was where we knew we both belonged.

My mother and Anne coped fantastically at home, Anne sleeping at our house and getting up to Hannah when she woke in the night. I did feel guilty about this but actually it was probably less upsetting for everyone that I stayed where I was. Sarah continued to feel better and started eating for the first time in days. By Thursday she was pining to go home and Dr Murray decided that that would be the best thing. She broke the good news to Sarah, who of course was delighted. She still doubted that Sarah would recover from her infection, so in fact thought it kinder to send her home.

We packed up all Sarah's things again and in addition to these we were given bedpans, disinfectant, a sheepskin rug for Sarah to lie on (as she had become so skinny) and also a wheelchair! This was to be a great success in the days that followed and gave Sarah that little bit of extra independence. We said goodbye to everyone, the staff so kind and obviously moved by the thought that they might never see Sarah again.

Simon had gone out and bought doughnuts for everyone and a box of chocolates, which Sarah gave the nurses, and a huge Snoopy card saying thank you.

It was so lovely going home and particularly special as we had never thought Sarah would come home with us again. Again we knew more and more how each day with Sarah was an extra blessing. Dr Murray came out to see Sarah two days later and was amazed at her rapid improvement. She was laughing and giggling and eating. It was hard to believe that less than a week ago they hadn't expected her to last through the night. I mentioned to Dr Murray that I wondered why God didn't let her die in hospital. But then God knows so very much better than us. How kind He was not to let her die then but to come home and spend Christmas and Stephen's birthday with us. Those last few weeks were so special to us as a family, and if God has ever showed us that He is looking after us and that all we need to do is trust Him, He was showing us then.

Sarah continued to improve so much and so quickly that it was decided that she could recommence her treatment. Originally, after her serious infection which so nearly killed her, there was no way she could have any more treatment, but as she was now so much better, almost miraculously so, it seemed best to give her some more treatment which they hoped would delay the leukaemic cells taking over. So on 17 November Sarah went in for more treatment and was able to return home early the following morning. She felt nauseous and was very sick again after it, but only for a day. She was so much stronger now and enjoying playing with her sisters at home. She resumed her lessons with her home tutor and enjoyed helping me in the afternoons looking after Hannah and Rebecca or cooking, which she was very good at. She was such a cheerful, helpful person and I really enjoyed her company and help. She had changed too, matured well in advance of her years. She said sometimes, 'I've changed, Mummy, haven't I?' or, 'My leukaemia has changed me,' and it was quite true. It had changed her.

But it wasn't so much having leukaemia that had changed Sarah, but the way in which God was changing her and gradually filling her more and more with His love. She had totally accepted her illness, she trusted God, and His love in her was becoming more evident. She had become more loving, more understanding, more patient and her deep love and trust in God was also strengthened. She was extremely happy, full of joy and not at all worried about her illness. Yes, Sarah was maturing and above all maturing spiritually. It was as if the gifts of her baptism had been strengthened within her. She had acquired a deep sense of sensitivity and also of responsibility to those around her. She would, for instance, get out of her own warm bed in the middle of the night if she heard Hannah crying in the room next to hers, and go in and see if she could comfort her. And in many other ways, she was so thoughtful towards us all.

We had long talks about everything and anything. Sarah was so easy to talk to and just a lovely person to be with. She was, in that respect, quite an exceptional child. Strangely enough, though, death was the one subject that we never did talk about. It just never came into the conversation. I am still glad that we didn't tell Sarah that she was going to die though deep down inside of me, in a way, I do wish that we had talked about it. Actually, this wish stems probably from selfish reasons, for I am sure that if she had known, it would have been Sarah who would have reassured us. There would have been no need for us to reassure her, for God was doing any reassuring that Sarah herself needed.

She took a great deal of pride in keeping her room neat and tidy, and she herself always appeared in the morning looking clean and neat. She was very warm and affectionate and most appreciative of anything and the last thing she ever wanted was to have anyone spend any money on her. Her lessons, now very often art work or her teacher simply reading to her, were super because Sarah did need time spent on *her*. But she started enjoying helping me look after Hannah and Rebecca again, reading them stories, getting them dressed or undressed and playing with them.

So for a short spell, our life resumed a fairly normal pattern, with hospital checkups slightly less frequent. We were so grateful for this time together and it was wonderful that Sarah was feeling so much better. Jenny and Rebecca especially enjoyed being able to play with her so much again.

We shall, of course, never know the extent of healing we all received through the Sacrament of the Sick. But one thing is quite certain. God touched us all in a very special way through this beautiful sacrament.

Sarah was just so much better both physically and also inwardly. Far from being close to death, she was now able to lead an almost normal life again, only days after there had been very little hope of her survival. But Simon and I too, were stronger. Our trust in God had been strengthened and we felt that He really was close at our sides, looking after us all.

10: Our loveliest Christmas ever

We knew at this stage that Sarah would be lucky to have another year to live but we were shattered when she relapsed again just at the beginning of December. It was the weekend of 4 December that she started feeling very tired and I noticed a few purpura—very tiny purple spots on her body. She was due to go to the hospital on Monday, so we went in, Sarah feeling so unwell that she lay down on a bed, half-asleep most of the time. This was most unlike her, for normally she would have been chatting and gigglng with the nurses.

Dr Davidson confirmed my strong suspicions. Yes, there were leukaemic cells in her blood again, and now we knew for certain that Sarah would have only weeks, if not days, to live. It was now 6 December—would she live until Christmas? This was the question at the back of all our minds. I prayed, we all did, that Sarah wouldn't die before Christmas, that God in His kindness would let her live and be with us for Christmas. Our prayers were to be answered.

Sarah was feeling dreadful all the way back home and got into bed as soon as we had returned. That afternoon she had been looking forward to going to her school to see the Christmas play, *Goldilocks and the Three Bears*. We were all specially invited that afternoon as it was the dress rehearsal and, as there would be no other spectators, it would be ideal for Sarah. She had been talking about the play for days and I knew she would be disappointed if she could not go, so I suggested she sleep for a bit and I would wake her up just before it was time to go. Also, for the first time, I gave her a spoonful of diamorphine to ease her pain and make her feel better. It certainly helped, although Sarah herself was so determined to go that she made a supreme effort to get up.

She was still feeling very ill in the car but by the time we reached the school she was feeling much better. This effort was rewarded beyond her wildest imagination; the children made her guest of honour; they even had a special little speech prepared for her, and it was obvious that they were thrilled she was there to watch.

We all thoroughly enjoyed the performance and at the end the headmistress, Sister Mary James, presented Sarah with a present from everyone, which touched us all deeply. Without even Jenny knowing, they had collected money and bought Sarah a radio. As I thanked Sister for such a lovely and generous gift she told me, 'If the Lord decides to take Sarah, then you can all have her radio.' I nearly said something, but bit my lip—no, we had decided to tell no one, so we must stick to it. But perhaps she guessed just how sick Sarah was, for she did look very pale and ill that day.

The afternoon, however, had given Sarah a tremendous boost. She had been so looking forward to returning to school, this was the first time since July, and she had really enjoyed the concert and seeing all her friends again. They were certainly very pleased to see her too.

In the days that followed Sarah grew noticeably more tired, and I started giving her diamorphine more frequently, which helped enormously. The Saturday after the concert was the hospital Christmas party for all the leukaemic patients and their families. We had all been looking forward to this and, thanks to diamorphine beforehand, Sarah joined in enthusiastically and we all had a super party. Her platelet count was so low that I was slightly worried that she might hurt herself, but she joined in everything, including musical chairs!

The Wednesday before she had been given more blood, and her hands were black and blue from the bruising where the drip had been put in. She was now starting to have bruises on her body, also more purpura. By the end she had so many spots that she was nearly covered in them. She was very upset as she noticed fresh patches of spots: 'Mummy, I've got more spots.' I reassured her, saying that she would be given some platelets which would help reduce the spots and, 'Anyway, Sarah, it doesn't matter what you're like on the outside. It's what's inside that counts,' I said.

The weekend before Christmas my father was organising a small party consisting of mostly family and close friends, in London. As we couldn't leave the children at home and under the circumstances I would never have left Sarah, he had very kindly arranged for us to stay at a Holiday Inn Hotel, complete with swimming pool. The children were very excited, both about going to London and staying in a hotel with a swimming pool. Simon and I, however, grew less and less happy about the idea of going to London at all as the week progressed. Sarah was rapidly going downhill; she certainly wouldn't enjoy the weekend feeling as she did, and at the back of our minds we both had the same fear—that Sarah would die in London.

The day before we were due to leave for our weekend, Sarah spent the day at the hospital having blood and platelets. Simon carried her to the car in the morning, as she was now too weak to walk, and he stayed with her all day, returning home with her in the evening. But when they arrived home we couldn't believe our eyes. Sarah, who had looked so frail in Simon's arms, actually *ran* from the car to the kitchen door. I threw my arms round her and hugged her.

We waited until Saturday morning before deciding definitely and then we prepared to go, with much apprehension but trusting in the Lord. We have come to the conclusion that this is the only thing you can do in such circumstances, but it still isn't easy.

Our weekend in London was memorable and the children really enjoyed staying in a London hotel. The swimming pool was incredible, London itself was beautiful with Christmas lights and decorations and we all enjoyed looking in the shop windows. But more than that, this weekend gave so many of the family a chance to see Sarah and her them, for the very last time (though of course no one was to know that till later on). It did help, when she died, for grannies, grandpas, aunts and uncles to have seen her so recently and that it had been such a happy weekend for us all.

On Monday morning, before we came home, we went shopping and bought a few new Christmas decorations and also some strawberries. The last few times Sarah had been in hospital having a drip put in I had told her to think about our weekend in London and all the things we'd do—and what would she really like best to eat? 'Strawberries,' she replied. So I promised her I would buy her strawberries, although she insisted they would be much too expensive. So buy her strawberries I did—knowing full well that she would never live to be able to eat them another summer. I was so thrilled to be able to buy them for her. Obviously I didn't care how much they cost; money really isn't important—we know that now.

We returned home; Simon and I were equally relieved to be going home and actually Sarah was too. It was now only five days until Christmas, and we started getting holly in and putting up simple decorations, also bringing in our Christmas tree and decorating it—something we all enjoy doing. It was so lovely all to be together and to share the preparations. We made Christmas biscuits and decorated these, the children helping to cut out the biscuit shapes and then icing them when they were cooked, and decorating them with hundreds and thousands, smarties and silver balls.

We strung our Christmas cards up on the low beams in our sitting room and the girls helped me make a simple holly wreath to hang on the back door, using holly, yew and ivy and a couple of red Christmas balls. Finally, we got our crib out of its box and unwrapped the crib figures from their tissue paper. We collected a bit of straw and greenery and arranged the figures in the little stable that Simon had made a few years before.

The Tuesday of that week, we had Mass in our house, a very simple and lovely house Mass. In recent years it has become fairly common to celebrate Mass in people's houses. This is how Mass would have been celebrated in the early church so, far from being something new, it is in fact a very early tradition that has recently been revived.

In our own parish, it was usual to have a house Mass each week during Advent. Parishioners were asked to say if they wished to have a Mass celebrated in their home and as far as possible, Mass was said in each area of the parish, giving everyone a chance to attend one of the house Masses if they wished. So as well as our own family, several other Catholics who lived nearby joined us.

We had pushed the chairs back in our living room to make more space. The smaller children sat on the floor at the front. We had placed a small table to be used as an altar at one side of the room. On the other side was our Christmas tree, with its lights and decorations and, on another table at one side, our crib.

One of the loveliest things about a house Mass is obviously the closeness and fellowship one experiences by being in a home, as opposed to a church. One immediately feels very close to everyone present, which is after all as it should be anyway, but that day especially was particularly moving and special.

Sarah, who wasn't really feeling very well, got dressed and came downstairs determined to join us. She read a bidding prayer she had made up, asking God to help all the children in the world but especially those who were poor, ill, sad or lonely.

Sarah was now going downhill fast, but we still hoped and prayed we would all be able to share Christmas together. She was now on diamorphine round the clock, when she was awake. It was hard getting the right dosage, enough to stop her feeling pain, but not giving her so much as to make her drowsy. She was also now suffering from headaches so on Thursday, Simon and I took her to Cheltenham where she was examined by two doctors. It was feared that the leukaemic cells could be returning to her brain, causing the headaches, and if that was the case Sarah would have to start more radiation treatment immediately. We were prepared for this, but it was to our and also to the doctors' huge relief that they decided this had not happened, and therefore we could return home. We were delighted.

Friday, Christmas Eve, I had decided that I wanted to buy Sarah a special Christmas present. My father was giving both Jenny and Sarah bikes for Christmas. I had tried to put him off giving one to Sarah, suggesting something more sedentary, but as I couldn't explain the position more fully the bike remained. Simon and I both knew that Sarah couldn't possibly ride a bike; she now needed to be carried nearly everywhere, though she did try to hobble, with some difficulty. I knew that she had always wanted a doll's pram and this now seemed a good idea. She had a Tiny Tears doll she was especially fond of and, even if she was in bed, I thought she would enjoy having her doll in a pram by her side. 'Don't you think she's a bit old for a pram?' Simon suggested but, 'No, I don't think so,' I said. I just had a strong conviction that this would be a very special present for Sarah. So on Christmas Eve, Jenny and I toured the shops of Gloucester to find a doll's pram, but returned home empty-handed—we had been unable to find one. Simon then went into Ledbury and reported back that there were a few in Tilley's. So off Jenny and I went; we walked into Tilley's and when we saw one particular navy-blue pram, it seemed to have Sarah's name written all over it. We paid for it and they put it inside a huge cardboard box. We were so excited about our find and could hardly wait for Christmas morning.

Simon's parents arrived that evening, having travelled over from Hertfordshire to spend Christmas with us. It was lovely to see them. We had a simple family supper together before they returned to their hotel in Ledbury. Then Simon and I, after tucking the children into bed, finished wrapping up parcels and had an early night.

Christmas Day dawned. It was to be a beautiful Christmas; on reflection I can see it was our very happiest and most peaceful Christmas ever, in so many ways.

Normally on Christmas morning we go to church after breakfast, return home and then open our presents before lunch. This Christmas, we decided we would open some presents at breakfast time. We didn't know how much longer Sarah would have and we wanted her day to be happy, and so the bikes from Grandpa were brought to the back door. Jenny and Rebecca were absolutely delighted naturally, but when Sarah saw hers her face fell, as we had feared it would. She started to cry. 'Don't worry, Sarah, we know you can't ride it yet,' we said, 'so come in the living room. We have a very special present just for you.'

Simon carried Sarah into the living room and sat her down in an armchair. Then he brought in her special present. She needed a little help to get it out, but when she saw it the joy on her face was indescribable. In fact, she was so happy that Simon and I both cried with joy. 'I've always wanted a doll's pram,' she said. 'Thank you so much, it's the very best present I've ever had.' She was over the moon, she needed no other present at all. She arranged her doll, dressed in the new babygrow from Jenny, under the covers and from that moment, except for going to church, her doll and pram remained at her side. Indeed, when she died her doll lay tucked up in the pram at the side of her bed. I cannot remember ever having been so pleased that I had done something that I felt I should. All day Sarah thanked us for her pram, saying that she had never asked for one because they're so expensive, and hugging us. Simon and I were both over-joyed at seeing her so happy.

We had arranged to meet Simon's parents at church and though Sarah was very wobbly, she insisted on walking up for communion. It was a lovely Family Mass. At the end of it Father Cashin said that this was one day in the year that we shouldn't worry about anything. 'Even if your turkey doesn't cook, don't worry,' he said. The Cameron family took these words to heart and remembered them especially that evening.

After Mass, Sarah went into the sacristy to say 'Happy Christmas' to Father Cashin who was going off for his annual holiday that evening. She cried when she said goodbye to him, and he too was deeply moved. Did she realise, I wonder, the significance of this goodbye. I feel sure that they both knew that they wouldn't see each other again.

We all returned home to our present-giving and lunch. After lunch Sarah had a long rest, then we laid the table for our Christmas dinner. However, when I looked at the turkey I had carefully stuffed and put in the oven five hours earlier, I was slightly dismayed to find that it wasn't nearly cooked! 'Never mind,' I said, 'Father Cashin said "don't worry, even if your turkey isn't cooked".' So we didn't, and enjoyed cold ham and mashed potatoes instead. We all agreed that it was the nicest Christmas dinner we had ever had!

How kind of God to allow us to share such a happy Christmas together! That night when we went to bed, Simon and I prayed thankfully to God for allowing us to have such a happy day. We had no need to fear, for He was truly looking after us.

On Sunday, Sarah's condition was deteriorating very rapidly. The spots all over her body had multiplied since she had seen Dr Murray on Thursday. I felt certain that she needed more platelets, and eventually rang the hospital as both Dr Murray and Dr Davidson were away. Staff Nurse was very kind, obviously sensing my concern and in the evening Dr Davidson rang and said he had organised for Sarah to go in, in the morning, to have blood and platelets. I was very relieved, especially about the platelets. So in the morning Simon and I deposited the other children at Anne's and took Sarah in together. It was without doubt the worst day we had ever spent in the hospital the whole time Sarah was ill, but at least we were together. Sarah was *so* tired and feeling very unwell. The drip would not go in—poor child, it wasn't surprising, her veins were so thin—but eventually they did manage to get it in and she had the platelets. The blood, when that arrived, kept on getting blocked up and wouldn't get through the drip. In the end, what should have taken a few hours took well into the night and eventually at ten o'clock the house doctor said she thought we should go home if we agreed, without the extra blood. Sarah had had some but it was such a job for it to go through the drip and Sarah was obviously distressed, so it seemed better to take her home. We agreed wholeheartedly.

Sarah was delighted to go home, but slightly disappointed that her extra blood hadn't made her feel much better. Nevertheless, she insisted on walking up to the ward with her doll in its pram to see the Christmas tree with its lights on and to say goodbye to the night staff. This particular set were Sarah's special friends; one nurse, Maggie, had stayed up reading to her one night until 3 a.m. Sarah hobbled rather than walked down the corridor to the ward. It was hard to contain my tears as I watched her, but I managed to, and gratefully cuddled her close to me all the way home. It was a cold but clear night, the sky was full of stars. As we were driving along, nearly home, Sarah suddenly said, 'Look at all the stars in the sky. If you see a shooting star it means someone is going to die, doesn't it?' 'Well, it does in the story of The Little Match Girl,' I replied, 'but not always.'

She was so pleased to be carried into the house in Simon's arms and up to her bed. We tucked her up, thanked Anne for putting the other children to bed, and then went to bed ourselves. For weeks now one of us had slept with Sarah. This night was my turn. We said our prayers and went to sleep. I was very tired and Sarah was too. Around 1 a.m. Sarah woke up ravenously hungry. She asked if she could have something to eat and I just thank God that I didn't suggest we go back to sleep, nor complain about getting up. In fact I quite happily got out of bed, put on my dressing gown and went downstairs. I made a tray of goodies for Sarah, homemade ginger bread, a banana and a glass of milk, which is what she had suggested. She was really excited with her 'midnight feast' and sat up in bed happily eating it. It was a lovely, unforgettable feast, and one which I, in particular, will never cease to thank God for. When Sarah had eaten her fill, we cuddled down again but now her arms and legs ached and she couldn't get back to sleep, so I told her stories of our wedding and honeymoon in Corfu, and eventually she went to sleep.

The next morning was Stephen's birthday. Everyone was excited and gathered in our room to give him his presents. That morning Rebecca and Jenny both got into Sarah's bed with her and wrapped up their present for Stephen together. He was delighted with his gifts, especially his roller-skate boots. Jenny had received roller-skate boots for Christmas from us, so they both skated together for quite some time that day.

Sarah was even tireder than normal and so full of affection for us. Several times that day she put her thin little arms around me, hugging me tightly, telling me how much she loved me and that I was the best Mummy in the whole world. She was also very affectionate towards Simon and we were delighted to return her warm embraces. I don't really remember that day very much, except that Dr Davidson came, just after Sarah had gone up to have a sleep. He popped up to see her and then came down and had a cup of coffee and a chat with us.

He left, promising to call again in two days' time. The weather was very mild and Jenny and Stephen enjoyed roller-skating. Sarah got up and we prepared and laid the table for Stephen's birthday supper. Normally we have birthday teas, but now the children are getting older and the elder three at least enjoy having supper with us, we decided to have a family birthday supper party. It was so lovely that we did, as it was to be our last family meal together. It was a very simple meal; cold meat, mashed potato, salad and the various party foods the children love—crisps, sausages on sticks and of course birthday cake, a Victoria sponge sandwiched with our own whipped cream and raspberries. The elder children had shandy to drink; Simon and I had wine. Even Hannah joined us in her high chair—it was a very happy family party. We sang 'Happy Birthday' to Stephen and we all looked forward to going out to lunch at a local bistro the next day for Stephen's birthday treat. At the end of supper, Sarah said that she felt '*so* tired', so I tucked her up into bed and soon cuddled down next to her, with Hannah.

We all fell asleep. Hannah woke around midnight and, fearing it would disturb Sarah, I took Hannah and climbed into our bed, Simon then going to 'cuddle with Sarah'. Rebecca also then woke up, so both Hannah and Rebecca landed up in bed with me. Around 4 a.m. I awoke to hear sounds from Sarah's room. I immediately realised that Sarah wasn't well and jumped out of bed to join Simon. We were both with her until the end.

11: Give me joy in my heart

Sarah died just before eight o'clock in the morning. It was a very peaceful death and looking back on it, I feel extremely privileged to have been there and also so grateful that she should die quietly in her own bed with both her parents at her side. The peace that surrounded us in her room was like a tangible presence.

We had both been with her since about 4 a.m. when she started being sick. Unknown to us, she had suffered a brain haemorrhage and her little body started thrashing about uncontrollably. So when this became worse, Simon had telephoned Dr Davidson. She had been complaining of a headache and, as she obviously couldn't have any morphine, we thought perhaps he could give her an injection. The thrashing about didn't worry us very much, as in the past when she had suffered migraine headaches she had had similar reactions.

So having wondered each night if she would die 'that' night, this particular night we had no idea that she was dying until the very end. She became unconscious quite quickly—but in our ignorance, we thought she was just asleep, until her breathing became very noisy, and then the realisation dawned upon us. We were grateful when her breathing became peaceful and when she died it was as though she was just fast asleep.

Left on our own in Sarah's room, Simon and I couldn't speak but just cried and clung to each other. Sarah was dead. We had known the inevitability of it for so long, but now it had actually happened we felt completely unprepared. We managed to pull ourselves together as we suddenly realised that the other children would soon be waking up. We rubbed our eyes dry, as best we could, and came out of Sarah's room. Dr Davidson and Lorraine, the nurse who had accompanied him, were standing on the landing. They, too, were very upset. We all came downstairs to the kitchen.

Just then I could hear Rebecca and Hannah waking up in our bed. Miraculously, this one special day of the year, they had not woken as usual between 6 and 7 a.m. Both Simon and I are convinced that this was no accident but God's great goodness to us, letting us be with Sarah on our own. I sometimes wonder how many angels were with us all that morning. Angelic presence was certainly evident in our house, keeping the little ones asleep, and in Sarah's room there was quite definitely a feeling of a heavenly presence and peace. How grateful we were to have been there.

Simon and I brought Rebecca and Hannah downstairs. Sweet little Rebecca had put her arm round Hannah to stop her falling out of our bed. My eyes welled up with tears. How do we tell the children that Sarah is dead? It will be such a shock to them. Yet we had to. 'Rebecca,' I said, 'you know we were talking about Heaven the other day? Well, Sarah has gone to be with Jesus in Heaven. She'll be so hapy there; she isn't ill any more.' I knew she couldn't really understand although in the weeks before Sarah's death I had talked to Rebecca about Heaven, trying to prepare her for this very moment.

Now we had to tell Jenny and Stephen. We tiptoed up their stairs. Stephen was fast asleep; Jenny was stirring but not yet fully awake. Dear, sweet Jenny—her twin sister dead. How my heart ached for her. The children had never even thought of the possibility of Sarah dying. We told Jenny and we all cried and hugged each other. We came downstairs and made a cup of tea, then we heard Stephen upstairs and went up to him. 'Stephen—Sarah died this morning. But she's in Heaven now. She was so very ill and she couldn't have got better and we know she's very happy now.' Stephen, too, burst into tears. The shock, the stark reality.

We gave each other strength that first day, in fact each day, and the strength we got from the children was quite amazing. After our cups of tea, Dr Davidson left, saying Dr Sims (our own G.P.) would call later to let us know what to do. A million questions flooded our minds. What do we do about the funeral, the body, how do we tell everybody? 'Look after your Mum,' Dr Davidson said to the children as he left. That dear, kind man—he was deeply moved and I think close to tears himself.

After he left, Simon and I looked at each other and both had the same thought—Anne, our very kind friend who had looked after any or all of the children at a moment's notice. 'I'll ring Anne,' I said. My voice was so choked up that she didn't instantly recognise who it was. 'Sarah died this morning,' I said. 'I'll be right there,' was her reply. She arrived and took Hannah and Rebecca home with her. What a super friend Anne was. She, too, was shattered at the sudden sad news, and it couldn't have been easy for her to have our children that day. I hadn't even got Hannah dressed yet. Jenny and Stephen opted to stay with us but perhaps to go down to Anne's later on.

We all wept together—then decided we ought to have some breakfast. Simon fixed us some scrambled eggs and we all forced them down. I'm sure it was the most difficult meal I've ever eaten, I could hardly swallow. Yet we knew we needed the nourishment that day. By about eleven o'clock Jenny and Stephen said they would like to go to Anne's, so Simon took them down. When he came back another good friend and neighbour, Andrew, arrived. He was so kind and in the days that followed was to be a pillar of support for us. Dr Sims arrived and Andrew left, saying he would call again later. Dr Sims, too, was very moved. He told us what we needed to do about contacting the undertaker and registering the death. I took him up to Sarah's room, let him in and again saw her frail little body—now empty, lying on the bed. I left him to write out her certificate of death on his own.

After he left we felt we must contact our family and friends. I had made a list of people to phone—starting with our parents. It was a formidable task. We so hated having to tell everyone; they would be so shattered. No one but ourselves had know Sarah was dying. But we had to do it. We took it in turns—first our parents, then friends. So many broke down on the phone and couldn't speak; you could hear their grief, their tears. We tried hard to console them. 'We had a very happy last few days. She died peacefully in her own bed, with us both at her side,' we would say. It hurt that we had to put them all through so much pain, but the fact that we could console them was a great blessing and one we are very grateful for.

We drank endless cups of coffee that day. Andrew returned to see how we were. He suggested an undertaker—a Mr Hawcutt, so Simon rang him and he came round very quickly. We both had a picture in our minds of a sort of Dickensian figure in a dark, shabby suit, but Brian Hawcutt didn't fit that description at all. We liked him from the first moment. A quiet, humble man—so kind and understanding. He carefully went through the questions he had to ask. It couldn't have been an easy task for him, but he was very patient. We must have talked with him for at least an hour, if not more. We took him up to Sarah's room. I had wanted her body to stay in the house, but he explained that it was a little difficult to do this, though possible, and described the chapel of rest, which sounded very nice, so we agreed that her body should go there and that it would be best to take her body right away, before the children came home.

That was one of the worst moments. Simon and I waited in the living room while Mr Hawcutt and Andrew carried Sarah's body down to his van. Dr Davidson arrived just as they were doing so; it was good to see him and extremely kind of him to come back again.

More telephone calls, and then Anne brought the children home. We bathed the little ones, gave them their supper and put them to bed. The older two stayed up with us for some time—they really were fantastically brave. Andrew arrived back and stayed; he was such a good friend and we were so grateful to him.

That evening I went into Sarah's room again for the first time since her body had been taken away. Her room was just as always; I couldn't believe she was really dead. I prayed earnestly to God, 'Give us the strength to cope. We know Sarah's happy with you, help us not to be too unhappy without her.'

That night and for many nights afterwards I woke up several times in the night and cried. We would sometimes cry in the daytime too; just simple things would set us off, like all of us being together—somehow there was such a void without Sarah, we seemed incomplete. But we tried hard not to cry and to be brave for the children's sakes and they in their turn helped us both.

The next few days were very busy, organising the funeral mostly—and that was a good thing as it helped to take our minds off our emotions and to concentrate on something practical. We knew right from the beginning that we didn't want a sad funeral. It wouldn't seem right. Yes, we were sad, and at times didn't know how we could cope, but all the same we were happy for Sarah. I felt totally convinced and Simon did too, as time went by, that Sarah was in Heaven, perfectly and blissfully happy, and it only seemed right to rejoice that she was no longer ill, nor in pain, but with God, where she belonged. We also knew that she would want us not to mourn but to be happy for her.

Simon and I pored over the New Testament in our efforts to choose two readings and also a Gospel. We had never read so many passages in such a short space of time. Initially, to our great dismay, we realised that Father Cashin, our parish priest, was not only on holiday but at an unknown location in Ireland. Therefore with no parish priest to guide us, we had to plan the funeral very much on our own. Added to this was the slight problem of bank holidays, as it was the New Year. However, the printers were fantastic and with our hymns chosen by Thursday lunchtime, they managed to print the service sheets ready for Monday morning, in spite of the bank holiday. The florists, too, were marvellous. We visited them and told them that we wanted simple but pretty flowers, also I particularly wanted some little posy arrangements on the centre aisles. These they did in yellow and white with white ribbons hanging down and they looked beautiful. I later discovered that they had spent the entire bank holiday not only doing all the flowers but also finding them, as so many wreath had been ordered.

The three nights prior to Sunday we had gone to the chapel of rest to see Sarah's body. The first night we took Jenny and

Stephen and although it was an emotional time for us all and very hard for them, we all felt so happy afterwards. The chapel of rest was a beautiful, very simple, peaceful chapel, with a few simple plants and Sarah's coffin, open, on the top. She looked so peaceful-her body so white. We had given Mr Hawcutt her woolly hat which he had put on her, also her special pillow which she always liked to sleep on, and a piece of pink Laura Ashley material to use as a sheet. We all knelt by the side of the coffin and prayed out loud, tears in all our eyes. Then we got up and first one, then another, bent to kiss her cheek. It was so cold, yet very soft. I had never seen a dead body before, let alone touched one. 'Mummy, she's smiling,' said Stephen. And she was. Yet to us all, in that moment, this small body was simply a shell. It wasn't Sarah. Sarah was elsewhere; this struck us all so forcibly and helped us considerably.

The next two nights, Simon and I went on our own to the chapel of rest, though especially on the third night we didn't really want to, it upset us both so much. We felt it was our duty, out of respect to that little body, and I'm glad now that we did.

I really felt the absence of Father Cashin. If I was ever starting to feel that God wasn't looking after us, it was now, with no parish priest to turn to for advice or even to talk to. But, as if in answer to our prayers, Father Campbell, a very old family friend and a priest I had known since childhood just happened to be on holiday in Cirencester and, on hearing of Sarah's death, he immediately drove over to see us. I was overjoyed to see him, as were Simon and Brian Hawcutt. I felt reminded of the words, 'Oh, ye of little faith,' which had certainly applied to me. I thanked God for being so kind, and determined to trust Him more.

Father Campbell had, in fact, offered Mass for Sarah on Christmas Day, and he said he would be delighted to officiate at her funeral. We explained our feelings about Sarah's death to him, in particular how we wanted a 'happy' funeral. He said we could choose any readings we liked and it was so good to talk to him and to know that he was there. We all felt much happier. We were also overjoyed and deeply touched to know that my Aunt Joan, a very special friend, and also my sister Helen, were both flying over from the States to be with us for the funeral.

The night before the funeral, Sarah's godmother, also called Sarah, her husband, Steve, and their ten-day-old baby daughter, drove all the way from Suffolk to be with us. It was super to see them and so kind of them to come all that way with their newborn baby. Actually, it was a marvellous distraction to our children to have them all with us, especially little Katie.

Simon and I had at last decided on our three readings by Sunday evening. We had also decided that we didn't want to be weepy bystanders, so intended to do the first two readings ourselves. Jenny and Stephen and two close friends would say the bidding prayers, which we jointly made up. And Stephen was to serve. With Father Campbell officiating, it was to be very much of a family service.

That evening, Simon and I and the elder two children had gone to the church with Father Campbell for the short and very beautiful ceremony of bringing Sarah's coffin into the church. It is fairly common in the Catholic church that the body is actually brought into the church the night before the funeral and stays there overnight. As the church is the family home of the parish, it signifies the moving from one part of the family (our family here on earth) to our family in Heaven.

Monday, 3 January, the day of the funeral broke—a grey, cloudy, rainy morning. 'Dear God,' I prayed, 'please couldn't it be a nice sunny day to cheer us all up?' But God knows what is best and it seems to me that he was gently showing us this all the time. A friend commented to me afterwards that the fact that the weather was so miserable was the best way of making the service that day really beautiful, by way of contrast. And she was so right. One does need darkness to appreciate light. So many people entered the church that day very sorrowful indeed, but left happier and more peaceful.

We got ready to go to church in a sort of daze and on someone's recommendation we had a few sips of sherry beforehand. Shirley, my super home help arrived, completely voluntarily, at 8.30 a.m. and spent the morning tidying up the house and getting ready for people coming back for lunch. A great number were coming from far away—France, Ireland, London, Hertfordshire and the Isle of Man, so we were to have quite a crowd back. Shirley also listened out for little Katie. It was so kind of her to come and I shall always be grateful to her for helping us that morning. In fact we couldn't have managed without her help those past few months.

Steve and our Stephen left early for church and we followed on with our friend Sarah in our car. As we were driving to church we prayed for strength to cope and not to fall apart. We wondered if there would be many people there, and for a moment thought how awful it would be if there were very few. As we drove up New Street in Ledbury, where the church is situated, we gasped at the rows of cars lining the road—could they all be for the funeral? We drove into the church carpark and got out of the car. Brian Hawcutt greeted us, then we slowly walked into the church together, with me carrying Hannah. Stephen met us just inside the church. It was the most incredibly moving sight I have ever experienced—the church was absolutely packed. Every seat was taken and people were standing at the back too. In fact I was told later that people were crammed into the little entrance hall and couldn't even get into the church.

We had seen the flowers the previous night, when we had gone to the church with Father Campbell for the very brief ceremony of bringing the coffin into church. They were so beautiful, and smelt so lovely, but with a crowded church they stood out and looked even more beautiful. And there in the aisle was Sarah's coffin—simple, beautiful and dignified. We silently walked to our seats at the front and the service started.

It was, without doubt, a truly beautiful service. Father Campbell said a few words at the beginning which put everyone more at ease. One of the loveliest things he said was that, 'Sarah doesn't have need of our prayers, for we are sure that she is now in Heaven, so rather than pray for her, I hope that she will now pray for me.' And I am sure that Sarah did pray for him.

Asking Sarah to pray for us doesn't mean that we prayed to Sarah in the same way as one prays to God. It means that we ask her to intercede for us, to ask God for us. In the same way as one asks one's friends and family to pray for you, while they are alive and on earth, it seems to me even more important to ask one's friends in Heaven to pray for us. They, being with God and filled completely with His love, are in a much more powerful intercessory position than anyone on earth.

When Father Campbell himself died suddenly just a few months later, we were saddened but happy to know that they were both now in Heaven and we felt sure that Sarah would have been one of the first to greet him.

The Mass began and it was so lovely. We were very pleased that we had decided to participate as it really was 'our' service and now we can look back on it as a lovely reminder to us of the joy we felt for Sarah. The voices were our voices, but the strength was God's, and I have never in my life been as conscious of His strength as I was that day. Many times since then I have read the words of Isaiah and they have given me great comfort and strength: 'Do not be afraid, for I am with you, stop being anxious and watchful, for I am your God, I give you strength, I bring you help, I uphold you with my victorious right hand.' (Isa. 41:10). And the strength that God was giving us all that morning was clearly evident. He was most definitely helping us and guiding us and holding our hands, and we felt the power of His love.

The Mass is, above all, a wonderful celebration of God's love for us. How grateful we were that God was helping us to celebrate this Mass in particular. We were so grateful for all the help He had been giving us, for all the love that He had shared with us and specially for giving Sarah to us. Now He was helping us celebrate her entry into Heaven, her being with Him, where she belonged.

All the children were fantastic; Stephen served with such reverence and composure; Jenny and her friends read their prayers out beautifully and even Hannah and Rebecca were as quiet as could be throughout the entire service. When Simon and I walked up to read our passages, I knew it was going to be all right and our voices were unfaltering.

Simon read first—a beautiful passage from St Mark's Gospel:

They brought children for Jesus to touch. The disciples rebuked them, but when Jesus saw this he was indignant, and said to them, 'Let the children come to me, do not try to stop them; for the Kingdom of God belongs to such as these. I tell you, whoever does not accept the Kingdom of God like a child will never enter it.' And he put his arms round them, laid his hands upon them, and blessed them. (Mark 10:13–16)

Sarah was a child, and the Kingdom of Heaven certainly belonged to her now. And to think that she was now in Heaven, that Jesus had touched her with His own hands and that now she was totally filled with His love and safe in the arms of her loving father in Heaven was fantastic.

But shouldn't we, too, be like children? It wasn't just because she was a child that Sarah was now in the Kingdom of God, but because she lovingly allowed Jesus to put His arms around her and lead her to a new life with Him. He had laid His hands on her, He had blessed her but she had to allow Him to work through her. She had to trust Him.

A child naturally trusts its father, but we too need to put our complete trust in God, our loving Father in Heaven who is leading us and guiding us all the time. He cannot force His love on us, though He readily offers it but we have to accept it and know that everything offered to us by Him is in some way a gift of love to us, a gift from His hands, a share in His kingdom.

My reading came from St Paul's letter to the Philippians:

I want you to be happy, always happy in the Lord, I repeat, what I want is your happiness. Let your tolerance be evident to everyone: the Lord is very near. There is no need to worry; but if there is anything you need, pray for it, asking God for it with prayer and thanksgiving, and that peace of God, which is so much greater than we can understand, will guard your hearts and your thoughts in Christ Jesus. (Phil. 4:4–7)

This is such a lovely reading. One can indeed be filled with joy in the Lord, even under the saddest or most difficult circumstances. Yes, we were sad that Sarah was dead, that she was no longer with us, but we could thank God for so many things, and as time went on, we could actually thank Him for the pain of losing her, and for the emptiness created by her loss becoming the space that He could fill with His joy and peace. In thanking God, we are assured by St Paul that we will receive peace, not peace as the world sees it necessarily, but peace in our hearts, given to us by God Himself.

I especially found the phrase 'the Lord is very near' meaningful, as at this particular time He was most definitely very near. Over the past few months, He had been making His presence clearer and clearer to us. The God whom we thought of in the past as a remote being, up in Heaven was in fact a living God, with us every single minute of every single day, a God who loves us, who wants us to be happy, who wants to fill us with His peace and His joy, a God who wants to share His own life with us, and we were becoming more and more aware of the many ways in which He had touched our lives with His love and with His strength.

Father Campbell then read the beautiful passage from St Matthew's Gospel where Jesus speaks of God's love for us and how we can trust Him to look after us, without being anxious about the future:

Therefore I bid you put away anxious thoughts about food and drink to keep you alive and clothes to cover your body. Surely life is more than food, the body more than clothes. Look at the birds of the air, they do not sow and reap and store in barns, yet your Heavenly Father feeds them. You are worth more than the birds! Is there a man of you who by anxious thought can add a foot to his height? And why be anxious about clothes? Consider how the lilies grow in the fields; they do not work, they do not spin, and yet, I tell you, even Solomon in all his splendour was not attired like one of these. But if that is how God clothes the grass in the fields, which is there today, and tomorrow is thrown on the stove, will he not all the more clothe you? How little faith you have! No, do not ask anxiously, 'What are we to eat? What are we to drink? What shall we wear?' Your Heavenly Father knows that you need them all. Set your mind on God's Kingdom and his justice before everything else, and all the rest will come to you as well. So do not be anxious about tomorrow, tomorrow will look after itself.' (Matt. 6:25–34)

This reading, telling us not to worry about anything material, seemed so relevant to me. Sarah had died but she had been raised up into new life with God. Surely it is not our lives now that are important, nor the material things of this world, but the life that God give us, His own life that He wants to share with us, that is important. The Kingdom of God, God's own life, is gradually growing within us. Since God Himself is the gardener, we do not have to worry about anything, for He knows exactly when and how to help us grow. But we have to respond by trusting Him, utterly and completely, and just as He gives the birds what they need without them asking for it, and just as the flowers are beautiful without doing anything on their own so, too, will we grow and blossom, if we hand over our lives to our Heavenly Father, and allow His love to take root in us.

And we don't have to worry about time. There is, after all, no time with God. We have to accept each moment, knowing that at each and every moment, God is supplying us with all the love we could ever need. Our job is to accept that love, in faith and trust, and leave the rest up to God.

All three readings were definitely pointing towards the same thing: that God our Father loves us, that He wants us to be filled with His joy, His peace and His love, that we need to trust Him and place our lives in His hands and then His love will grow in us.

The entrance hymn we sang reinforced those very things as we prayed for joy, love and peace.

God was certainly helping us that day and I was so grateful to Him. I think a great many people felt the presence of God with us all that morning, for the Holy Spirit was undoubtedly at work in so many ways, and His power very evident. A great number of people have since told us of the marvellous boost it gave to their faith to be present at Sarah's funeral. It certainly gave us tremendous faith to feel God helping us so much.

After the Mass was over, we followed the coffin out of the church. There were so many people at the back of the church and in the porch that it took some time. We got into our car, and as we were sitting there waiting to follow the hearse, I noticed Dr Davidson standing at the side of the church. He gave me such a lovely smile and acknowledgement as if to say, 'Yes, it was a beautiful funeral and it *has* made me happier.' This in turn made me feel happier too. We were so grateful for everyone's presence that day—and the love, support and prayers of all our friends and family has been a tremendous source of strength and comfort to us. But that day we were especially pleased to see Dr Davidson, Dr Murray and all the nurses who came from the ward, most of whom were on duty and came in their uniforms. That meant a great deal to us.

As we drove down the road very slowly behind the hearse, I felt all senses numbed and as we drew up at the graveyard, it was raining. The short ceremony of interment was quickly over. I was glad we didn't sprinkle earth onto the coffin, nor were the words 'dust to dust' used. Instead there was a very simple, short blessing and it was all over. I thought this would be the worst part of the ceremony, but for me it wasn't, though I know it was for Simon. People came up to us from all sides, shaking our hands and embracing us, then we climbed into our car to shelter from the rain and drove home.

Family and friends came for lunch—I was pretty dazed now that the funeral was over, and if it hadn't been for sensible relatives and friends I'm sure no one would have got anything to eat.

We particularly wanted to see all the flowers on the grave, so we returned at about four o'clock, before it was dark. They were so beautiful, and there were so many of them. We returned home, still numb from everything that had happened, but so grateful to God for not letting us fall apart and for making Sarah's funeral service so beautiful and so meaningful to so many people.

That night we prayed and in particular, we asked Sarah to pray for us all: that we would have strength to carry on as we knew she would want us to; that we would have strength to accept God's will in our lives, as she had done in hers; and that she would help us know that she really was happy and in Heaven.

As a Catholic, I believe in the Communion of Saints which means that we are all part of the Body of Christ. When people die, this does not cut them off from the Body of Christ, on the contrary, in Heaven they become even more powerful members, firstly because they are with God, and secondly because they are totally and completely filled with the love of God. So we pray to our brothers and sisters in the Body of Christ who are in Heaven, to help us on our journey. That is why we prayed and still do pray to Sarah and not only do we feel that her prayers for us are very powerful, we also feel that she would want to pray for us, and to help us.

The days immediately following the funeral were not easy and we were all wandering around, I suppose, in a state of delayed shock. There had been so much to do and now it was all over. Everything seemed very empty and we felt very lonely without Sarah. But we had the other children to think of and so tried to be brave for their sakes, and our natural feelings of sadness and grief bound us all very closely together.

We were grateful for the visit of my aunt the following Monday. It was just for two days but it was good to see her. After Aunt Joanie left, Jenny had to go back to school again—no easy task for her, but we felt she would be better off getting back into a normal routine as soon as possible, and the activities and friends at school would be better for her than being at home without Sarah. From that point of view we were lucky; as Sarah hadn't been at school at all since July, Jenny was at least used to going to school without her. It was the coming home that was hardest in those earliest weeks. It must have been so lonely for Jenny, and my heart ached for her. It also ached for Rebecca, who was so accustomed to having Sarah at home and loved her so much. Sarah had always been very kind and patient with Rebecca, besides being unusually sensible and responsible. Before Sarah became ill in July, Rebecca's morning ritual consisted of climbing into our bed around 5.30 a.m. and then climbing into Sarah's as soon as we heard her awake an hour or so later.

So our hearts truly ached for ourselves, for each other and for the children. Sometimes my eyes would well up just thinking of Sarah, and it was really hard to keep back the tears. Simon and I did manage to help each other. But as the days wore on it all seemed harder and the grief became more acute. I suppose this is because at the beginning we were numbed by the shock and, as this numbness gradually wore off, we were faced with the stark reality that Sarah really was dead, not with us any more, and all that this meant to our lives.

As well as missing her so deeply we also felt a very strong sense of emptiness caused by suddenly not being as busy as we had been. While Sarah had been ill we had to think continually, of giving her her tablets and in the final days, her morphine too. Did she have a temperature? Should we phone the doctors? Would we need to leave the children somewhere today? We had also tried as much as possible to do things with Sarah—play games with her and especially read to her. Thus the void of not needing to worry about her and not having to look after her was in itself very apparent and took several months to get used to.

I thanked God so much for the other children. I was lonely

in the daytime with just Hannah and Rebecca, but at least I had them—how much worse for a parent with no other children, I thought. Even when as a family we sat down to a meal together there was a big gap, all too noticeable and that gap is still there months later and, I suppose, will always be there. But it is no use looking on the bleak side. Yes, it does still hurt. The grief of bereavement is something that you cannot appreciate unless you have gone through it. We thought we knew what it was like, but we had no idea until we experienced it what a deep, lonely, heart-breaking feeling it is.

The hospital, doctors and nurses had been so much a part of our lives that we *needed* to keep in contact—just so that all ties with Sarah weren't immediately severed. It helped a lot to go in and see them all; we did so the week after the funeral and were pleased we did. However, the next time we went, I found it very hard—as thoughts flooded back of Sarah's treatment, so many days and moments now all gone, and Sarah gone too. It can still be hard when we drive to Gloucester, but now I want to remember every single little detail.

12: Thunderbolts

After Sarah died, Simon and I fortunately seemed to go through severe experiences of grief alternately, and we would console each other by saying, 'Don't worry, Sarah is happy.' I was content to accept that she was, but Simon needed more than that—he wanted proof, a sign from Heaven. So each day we prayed that God would show us both, and Simon in particular, that she really was happy.

Our prayers weren't just answered once, but time after time until after about five months, Simon no longer doubted but was absolutely convinced both of the existence of God and of Heaven. This, in itself, was a wonderful gift from God and one which has made us both very happy and has given us much strength.

We received so many 'thunderbolts', as we called them, from God, but two in particular stand out in my mind. The first happened in March, just a week before Jenny's tenth birthday. It was a particularly difficult time for us all, as this was going to be Jenny's first birthday on her own, without Sarah. We had told Jenny's school that we wanted to give them something in Sarah's memory and we were delighted when Sister Mary James, the headmistress, suggested a magnolia tree. We obtained one and also a very simple plaque to go underneath it. Sister then arranged a little tree-planting ceremony, inviting Dr Davidson and some of the nurses from the hospital, Father O'Connell, the school parish priest, and also our family.

We were to plant the tree during a simple ceremony and at the end of it Sister was going to hand over a cheque to Dr Davidson for £400, which the school had raised for the leukaemia unit at the hospital, a marvellous total for a small school. The day before the tree-planting ceremony, the weather was cold and rainy and the day itself was exactly the same. 'Please, Sarah,' we said, 'let it be fine this afternoon.'

Dr Davidson and some of the nurses had lunch with us at our house and then we all drove off to Ross in the rain. It was incredible—Simon noticed it first, as we were driving towards Ross on the motorway, you could see the sun coming out through the clouds and shining directly onto Ross itself. When we arrived at the school, five minutes later, the rain had stopped and it was no longer cold, in fact it was more like a spring day!

All the children were assembled outside. The short ceremony was simple and beautiful. We had thought that it would be a very emotional time for us, but it wasn't. We were welcomed by one of the children. Simon then planted the tree and Father O'Connell blessed it. At this point, his dog, who nearly always accompanies him, started rolling about on the grass and Hannah started giggling. This, in turn, brought smiles and also a number of giggles from the children. It was so lovely—I'm sure Sarah was giggling too! The children then sang a lovely hymn and Sister presented the cheque to Dr Davidson, who was most appreciative and said a few words of thanks.

The short ceremony over, we were taken into the staff-room and given a glass of sherry. While we were standing chatting, one of the teachers, whom Sarah had been especially fond of, remarked on the fantastic change in the weather. 'Yes,' I agreed, 'but do you really think Sarah would have let all those children stand out there in the pouring rain!'

Jenny's birthday, the following week, was again marked by this beautiful spring-like weather. It wasn't just sunny, but warm, and all the children were outside playing till 6 p.m. Again, we had asked Sarah to help us all that day and we were so grateful for such lovely weather on those two occasions.

The second 'thunderbolt' was in connection with a draw which our local Round Table helped to organise. We wanted to raffle Sarah's bicycle (her unused Christmas present), and to give this money to the hospital too. Over three and a half thousand tickets had been sold and the draw took place at a cheese and wine evening, organised by the Round Table, the proceeds of which were also going to the hospital.

Nearly all the nurses from Sarah's ward had come to the cheese and wine evening, and of course Dr Davidson too. He had kindly agreed to give a short talk about children with leukaemia and how the money would help, and this talk was extremely interesting and very well received. After his talk he had been asked to draw out the winning tickets.

Simon and I had prayed so hard about the draw and in particular about the person who would win Sarah's bike. We so wanted the bicycle to go to someone who needed it and prayed that this would happen. So we stood awaiting the result of the draw with great interest and a certain amount of apprehension. We nearly fainted when Dr Davidson read out the name on the winning ticket, 'Mrs Cain'. Now, Mrs Cain's husband, Cecil Cain, had died just a few weeks before Sarah. He had been very ill for some time and when Sarah was so very ill in November, Father Cashin had asked him to pray for her. He had also asked Sarah to pray for Mr Cain, which she did. In fact, she very much wanted to visit him but never had the opportunity before he died. So Sarah and Mr Cain had never met, but had prayed for each other and when Sarah died Brian Hawcutt, who knew of this, asked us if we would like Sarah to be buried next to Mr Cain. It wasn't actually the next plot but it could easily be arranged. We thought that it was a lovely idea and so Sarah was buried next to Mr Cain.

How marvellous it was then when Mrs Cain won Sarah's bike! If anything was ever a sign from Heaven, this seemed to us to be a very positive one. And it gave Mrs Cain a fantastic boost as it did us. We were even more delighted when Mrs Cain later asked us if we would mind if she used Sarah's bicycle towards raising money for a hospice for the terminally ill, which is being built locally, which would have helped her husband so much if it had been built in his lifetime.

So not only did Sarah's bicycle raise money for the leukaemic children in Gloucester, it was also helping to raise money for the hospice near Hereford. It certainly seems to me that both Mr Cain and Sarah helped, not only in showing us that they are both in Heaven, but how pleased they must be to be able to help patients suffering from illnesses similar to their own.

There is one other incident which, though not really a thunderbolt, certainly ought to be mentioned here. It was something that impressed me, in particular, as specially lovely.

The night that Sarah died, our American friend Angela had an extremely vivid dream. She dreamed that Sarah was dancing. Now Angela hadn't dreamed of us before so it was certainly rather strange that this particular night she dreamed of Sarah and only of Sarah. Furthermore, Angela was four thousand miles away, in the United States. But with the time difference it meant that in the middle of the night when Angela was asleep and dreaming, it was morning our time, and Sarah died at 8 a.m.

Angela was just as amazed as we were to realise that when she dreamt of Sarah dancing, Sarah was probably doing precisely just that: dancing with joy in Heaven!

13: Our own special angel

Since Sarah's death we have thought a great deal, talked a great deal and prayed a great deal. We have, for the first time in our lives, come face to face with death and a death which in the eyes of many people is a tragic one. But was Sarah's death tragic? More and more I am convinced that it was anything but.

Sarah's actual death was very peaceful and free from pain. She died in her own bed (which is where she would have wanted to die), with both her parents at her side. We are so grateful for that and also for the happy times we spent together as a family those last few months, in particular for our holiday in September, being together for my birthday, our fantastic weekend in London, our lovely Christmas and Stephen's birthday the day before she died, when we shared his birthday supper together in our kitchen.

Then we were so grateful that Sarah didn't die in November, and there was certainly no medical reason to account for her recovery. Talking to Dr Murray one day, some time after Sarah died, I asked her if she thought it was a miracle that Sarah didn't die in November. I know the medical staff thought that she was going to die then and we thought that it was a miracle, but what I didn't know was that after Sarah's CHOP treatment, when she became so ill, she had virtually no white cells in her body at all. And apparently, there is no recorded case of anyone surviving with so few white cells in their blood! Dr Murray was quite certain that it was a miraculous recovery. In His great wisdom, God had not only allowed her to live to be with us for Christmas and Stephen's birthday, but knew that our faith needed this. Simon and I also consider that we were so lucky knowing that she was going to die and having the chance of making her last few weeks, and also our family life, as happy as possible. At least we can have no regrets about wishing we had done something differently.

The fact that Sarah's short life was a happy one is an added blessing, and she had also given a great deal of happiness to other people. She taught us so much about patience, trust, kindness, love and acceptance, and her death has taught us much about God and His love for us. She reached out to so many people both in her short life and by her death, so she certainly did not die in vain. We all have a job to do in life and it seems to me that Sarah did hers extremely well. I think perhaps that even her death was part of that job—it has certainly changed our lives and also the lives of many other people.

Father Campbell pointed out to us that because we measure everything in time, we think it is sadder when a young person dies. However, if one believes in Heaven, then surely the time-span on earth is irrelevant. What is important is getting there.

Death is still a taboo subject. People avoid talking about it, which is understandable. Why should you think about death when you are busy thinking about life? I suppose, also, that in our society today, modern medicine has made death something which can often be deferred, and certainly death in children is comparatively rare. Many people are embarrassed and possibly also frightened of death and avoid the subject, not wanting to hurt your feelings or simply not sure what to say. Certainly, we had never thought much about death until Sarah died. It is only when death meets you head on that you are able to realise that death is a very real part of life. In fact, coming to terms with death makes life more meaningful.

Our priorities in life have changed. We realise so much more clearly that material things are not important, nor is status, position or wealth. You don't take your overdraft with you when you die, nor your nice car or new carpet. You do take what's inside you and *that* is what is important. We have learnt the hard way but we needed to learn it and are grateful that we did, that what really matters is our day-to-day relationships with our family, our friends and the people we meet, how we make the best use of the gifts and talents we have and also how we make the best use of the time we have, for our time will run out.

Yes, death will one day come to us all. It is the one sure thing that we know will happen to each and every one of us. Yet we avoid talking about it. It is something unknown and something we have to do on our own, so it can be frightening. Sarah's death has shown us that death need not be frightening. We are so sure of God's love for us now that we are no longer afraid of death, for death in a way is going home, and knowing that Sarah will be there to help us, when we do die, is very comforting.

Sarah was such a happy, loving child. Why, people ask, does God, if there is a God, allow children to die? Why does he allow suffering, unhappiness, war? If there were a God, then He wouldn't allow such things to happen, or if He does, then how can He be kind and loving? I don't think that we can understand all the answers to such questions. Yes, sad things do happen. Our world is full of the most dreadful, terrible things, some of which happen as a result of man's own free will, others just seem to happen. But I don't think we can say there isn't a God just because such things happen. For me, it points even more strongly towards God.

Yes, there is something more, something better than suffering, sadness, war, death. And it is Good News! News that we sang about at Sarah's funeral: 'How lovely on the mountains are the feet of him who brings good news.' And the Good News is that there is a God who loves us and is looking after us all the time. God isn't some unreachable entity up in Heaven but a loving Father who is with us here and now.

Just because Sarah became ill and then died does not point to the fact that there is no God, nor that if there is, that He can't be very kind. I believe that sometimes God allows things to happen *because* he loves us and Sarah's death was part of His loving plan for us. For Sarah, being so ill and going through so much, brought her very close to God and prepared her for Heaven. There was so much love in Sarah and it grew when she was ill. She set us all a fantastic example, as she trusted God with her child's simplicity. 'Do you think it would help if I prayed?' she asked Dr Murray, in November, when Dr Murray was explaining about having to get white cells for her. Sarah trusted God even when it meant being seriously ill, having unpleasant and sometimes painful treatment, when it meant losing her pretty hair, not being able to see her friends. What was so fantastic was that the love and strength that shone from within her became visibly stronger and stronger as her body became weaker. Those last few days before she died she was so very close to God and ready to go to Heaven. She seemed 'heavenly' and looking back on it, I think that she knew that she was soon going to be with God. If I ever felt close to God, it was being near Sarah those last few days and particularly when she actually died. 'An angel has touched me . . .' my aunt wrote to us when Sarah died and yes, that was how we felt too.

For us, the grief, loneliness and sadness all made us open to God. It has made us reach out to Him and He has responded over and over again to our cries for help. He has shown us that He does love us. Sarah's death was not something that happened by chance. God allowed it to happen.

Now, as I write this, I am only too deeply aware of other people's grief and suffering, so much of which is far, far greater than mine. All I can offer is my own personal experience, not measuring it against anyone else's. All I want to say is that I believe that God has shown us that He has been, and still is, beside us every step of the way. We have coped, not because we have been able to, but because God has helped us to do so. The strength is not our own—but His, which He gives freely if we ask for it.

However, when our lives are progressing fairly smoothly, with no more than occasional ups and downs, we manage (or think we can manage) fairly well on our own. God is there all the time but we don't feel we need Him. Only when something happens which makes us suddenly realise that we can't cope on our own, do we find out that we need God and ask for His help. I think that so often we *need* this to happen. It was certainly true of us. Before Sarah was ill, we didn't really think we needed God. It was only when we discovered that she had a potentially fatal disease that we realised that we couldn't cope on our own and so we turned to God. The more difficult the situation became, the more we found that we turned to Him and that we had to trust Him, knowing that He is in control.

When Sarah was ill, this meant trying not to worry about what was going to happen and just taking each day at a time. It meant trusting that God knows what is best and then trying to do our best, knowing that He would help us. It meant leaving the worrying to Him and spending our time and effort in looking after our family. 'Why worry, when you can pray,' Father Cashin said one Sunday. This thought struck me very deeply and it has come to my mind many times since I heard it. I have always been a worrier but really one achieves nothing positive by worrying—apart from frayed nerves, insomnia and ulcers. But prayer really does help. We have found that it can be a great source of strength and comfort, and praying together has bound us closer together too. I, for one, never truly valued the power of prayer until Sarah became ill. So many people prayed for us all during that time and also when she died. We could at times actually feel the tremendous power of prayer, the most incredible sense of strength and love, which in turn also brings peace and joy.

Since Sarah's death, we have experienced various emotions, most of which have, I believe, followed a fairly normal pattern of bereavement. Firstly, there was the numb shock of it all, so deep that it is impossible to grasp, but so very real. Gradually, however, this initial numbness wore off and the stark reality became clearer and clearer: Sarah really was dead, she wasn't coming back. Then the tears, the sleepless nights, the emptiness in the house, specially in her room, the empty space at the kitchen table at meal times, and missing her in so many other sorts of ways. We thought we would be prepared for this and I suppose in a way we were, but it was only when we came face to face with death that we could appreciate the depth of grief and pain caused by that kind of separation, and of the void it leaves in one's life.

Time doesn't really heal, but God can, and I am sure that He wants to do so. He has shown us so many times from the very beginning when Angela came to us, throughout Sarah's illness, but perhaps even more so since her death, that He is there all the time. He has helped us not only to accept Sarah's death, but to realise that death is not the end of life but the beginning of a new life with Him. Only by dying can we fully partake of that life, so really it is a triumph—a cause for celebration.

Simon and I are now both totally convinced that Sarah is in Heaven. Made by God, because He loves her, she is now with Him, no longer ill, nor in pain but perfectly and utterly happy. When I think of all the drugs and injections, all the tablets she had to take, all her headaches and tiredness and nausea and other aches and pains, it makes me so happy to know that she is now free from all that, and instead so perfectly happy.

Our grief is for ourselves, our family and others around us. And it is real—very real. We still miss Sarah dreadfully and I'm sure we always shall. Believing in God and His love for us doesn't make it any easier, nor does it gives us a cushion to bury our heads in, but it allows us to use our grief. With God's help, therefore, it can become something positive that we can grasp and use. It can help us to mature—and to grow away from ourselves and closer to God. Joy and blessings can and do come out of the depth of sadness, grief and suffering.

For me the last two months prior to Christmas and the first anniversary of Sarah's death, were some of the most difficult and most painful in the whole year since her death. At the beginning, just after she died, eight o'clock in the morning was the most difficult time, then each Wednesday and as the weeks progressed, each 29th of the month brought fresh feelings of intense grief. However, from July onwards, we automatically thought back to 'this time last year' and so, from October onwards, which is when we first knew she would die, I found myself getting easily depressed, not in the least joyful, self-pitying even and bitter, something which up until now we hadn't experienced at all, but all part of the normal pattern of grief. The more intense the feeling of grief, the more I turned to God, trusting, hoping, praying that He would help. I was dreading Christmas and the anniversary of her death, so I prayed all the more.

One Sunday in church the organist started playing *For all the Saints* and when everyone started singing all I could do was break down in a flood of tears, for that was the final hymn we had sung at Sarah's funeral, as the coffin was carried out of church.

My grief didn't seem to get any better but then suddenly, just before Christmas, I was filled with the most beautiful and intense feeling of joy and peace. And instead of thinking of how much we were missing Sarah, I was struck with the thought of how fantastic it must have been for Sarah when she entered Heaven for the first time; how radiant she must have been, how excited, overjoyed and so happy to be among God's family, meeting relatives she had only heard about, meeting other local children who had died and of course meeting Mr Cain, for whom she had prayed. How happy she must have been meeting Mary, but above all, seeing and being with Jesus and God the Father in all their glory.

These beautiful thoughts erased all sadness from within me and I felt myself rejoicing! *Give me joy in my heart* we had sung at Sarah's funeral. Yes, we had prayed for joy and peace, and so many people had prayed for us for those very same gifts. Now I understood a little bit of what those wonderful gifts mean and I thanked God for them with all my heart.

So Christmas was a happy time. We missed Sarah but amidst the pain of not having her with us was also the joy of knowing that she was happy, and with that joy came that peace of Christ, which only God can give.

Shortly after Sarah died, someone told us that he thought that the greatest miracle of all was that Simon and I were still smiling. I think perhaps that he was right. More than anything I can thank God for letting us smile and for inwardly giving us peace; for letting us know that Sarah is happy; for helping us in so many ways during her illness and since her death; for all the kind friends and relatives who have been so supportive in so many ways; for the many wonderful people we have met and most especially for the hospital staff. I can thank Him too for changing our priorities in life and for showing us that what is important is what's inside us. I thank Him for helping us grow closer together as a family and that Simon and I have grown closer, not only to each other, but that together we have grown closer to Him.

Sarah's death has been sad, yes, but full of blessings. Deep down in our most painful feelings of grief and sadness, we have found joy and hope and love. We have found God. More than anything else, Sarah's death has made us open to God. Her death has most definitely been the very saddest thing that has ever happened to us. Most people, I am sure (and ourselves included), would regard the death of one of their children as one of the very worst things that could ever happen to them. Although certainly the very saddest, Sarah's death has actually been one of the best things that has happened to us. Without it, we would still be drifting through life. We would be worrying about things that aren't really important at all, not really sure of what *is* important.

Death makes you ask yourself questions you possibly had never asked before. It makes you want to know why you're here at all. What should you be doing while you're here? Where are you going when you die? If Sarah hadn't died we certainly wouldn't have thought much about any of these questions. Nor would we have realised that we can't manage on our own. We wouldn't have reached out to God as we did from the depths of our grief and loneliness and found that not only is He there, He is the very reason for our existence. In our darkness, He became our light. We need Him and He is always there beside us.

Sarah, in a way, is our own special 'angel', sent to us from God to lead us towards Him. But having been led towards Him, we still have a long way to go! And the road will not be easy. We know now, though, that God will be beside us all the way. Sarah, now happy in Heaven with God, will help us too.

'Sarah will look after her family better than any guardian angel,' Father Campbell wrote, in a letter to us shortly after her funeral. We know that she will.

14: How lovely on the mountains

I wrote most of the first part of this book in the year after Sarah died. I had wanted to try and share how her death itself had brought us so very much closer to God and also to try and show how we felt that God had quite definitely been looking after us and helping us in so many different ways.

Now, a year later, I am writing the last chapter. Just as Sarah experienced new life when she died, we too, have experienced and still are experiencing new life. We are also coming to understand a little better the meaning of that new life. My own experience since Sarah's death had led me farther along the journey into that new life. And it is so wonderful that again, I would like to share my thoughts and experiences with you.

Sarah is now at the end of her journey: ours has only just started. So although this is the final chapter, for us, it is also the beginning . . .

Before Sarah became ill, I read two books by Merlin Carothers about praising the Lord in every situation in life, even in adverse circumstances, and how doing so releases the power of God to work, precisely in those circumstances. These two books made a very deep impression on me and I reread them while Sarah was ill. Although the idea of praising God seemed right and I did trust that God was looking after us all, I just could not then bring myself to praise God for Sarah's illness. To have done so, at that time, would have seemed to me to be saying that I was glad that she was ill, and I certainly wasn't glad at all.

But after Sarah's death, this idea of praise kept on coming back to me and the more I thought about it, the more I began to see that yes, I *could* praise God for everything that had happened, not because I was glad that Sarah had contracted leukaemia and had died, but just because God is God and His love for us is so great, so incredible, so everlasting.

So I started to praise God for absolutely everything that had happened and most of all I praised Him for Sarah herself. I praised Him for her short life with us, for each and every moment of that life. And I praised Him for her illness and for her death too. For it is precisely through her death that we have come to see that God loves us, that we need Him, that what is important is His life growing within us. We have come to see that God is not someone who is far off, up in Heaven, who sometimes listens to our prayers, and sometimes answers them the way we want them answered, but a very real Father who loves us and is at our sides all the time ready to help. He doesn't always help in the way we think is best for us but He knows so much better than us what is best for us and He loves us so much, that we can trust Him.

But we needed to be broken in order to turn to Him and ask for His help. It is precisely when we are broken that God can enter into our lives and transform them with His presence, and fill them with His love, so that His Kingdom may grow within us. Like the grain of wheat that has to die, we needed to be broken in order to open ourselves to God's love for us and allow him to share His life with us. In our brokenness, not only did we become aware of our need for God and our utter dependence on Him, we became aware of our need for His strength in our weakness, His light in our darkness, of His help when we felt so utterly broken. And God in His great love did share our burden and did give us His strength. It was then that we realised that our need for Him is far, far deeper than the need for strength to cope in a difficult situation. He is life itself, He is love itself and without Him, we are nothing.

Our brokenness helped open our eyes and through it we are just beginning to see and to look away from ourselves and look towards God. Our brokenness has created a space that God can fill and is filling with His own life and with His love. His love does not necessarily take away the pain. On the contrary, Jesus frequently told His disciples that to follow Him was not easy, that to follow Him you had to 'take up your cross'. But we do not take up our crosses on our own. All through Sarah's illness and even more so since her death we have coped, not with our own strength but with the strength given to us by God, and the deep void in our lives is gradually being filled with His peace.

So we can praise Him and thank Him for our sorrow and grief, we can praise Him for Sarah's death, for it made us reach out to God and thus enabled Him to respond by sharing His strength, His love and His life with us.

Just as God had become more real to me as a loving father, so too, was He becoming more real to me in Jesus Christ, His son. And I was beginning to glimpse the wonderful truth that God wants to give us all new life, He wants to share His own divine life with us. In glimpsing this incredible mystery, I was also beginning to understand better the mission of Jesus, God the Son. And I realised that as we had reached out in our grief and had found the arms of God our Father supporting us, so too, had we found the arms of Jesus stretching out to us from the cross. And I realised that in the very depths of our grief, in the very depths of our sorrow, God was actually there with us all the time, for God Himself became Jesus Christ, the Man of Sorrows.

For Jesus, the cross meant suffering and death but it also meant resurrection and new life, and so too, I believe, can we find new life in the depth of sorrow and in the depth of what the world would call a tragedy. When Jesus died for us on the cross, He gained a total, absolute victory for us over sin, over death, over suffering; a victory that is everlasting. Our God reigns over all suffering, all death and there is nothing that can take away His incredible love for us: a love we don't deserve or earn but a love that chose us to be His children, His own sons and daughters, knowing our weaknesses and sinfulness and loving us in spite of them. However, man said 'no' to God Sand in doing so, rejected life itself and chose death, which is separation from God. But even after man rejected God, God still loved man, so much so that God

Himself became a man and died for us, so great is His love for us, so that we, in turn, might not die but could have new life through Him. His death brought the resurrection and, with it, new life for all. Our death too, now means new life, because death is no longer the end of life but the beginning of new life, glorious life, united with our God.

> *Dying you destroyed our death*
> *Rising you restored our life,*
> *Lord Jesus come in glory.*

And I praise and thank God for the new life He gives us, that Sarah now shares with Him in Heaven and that one day, we too, hope to share. But He has invited us to share in that life *now*.

When we pray 'Thy kingdom come, thy will be done, on earth as it is in Heaven,' I didn't realise until fairly recently that we are, in fact, praying that God's Kingdom will come and in fact, *is* coming on earth, here and now. Just as Sarah is sharing in the Kingdom of God in Heaven, we also can share in His Kingdom here on earth, for the kingdom of God is within us. I had always known, or at least I thought I knew, that through our baptism we have become God's own children, that we are given a share in God's own life, but somehow the words had never really sunk in. I had never realised what it means to say 'Our Father'. Now for the first time I was beginning to become aware of the fantastic truth that yes, God is *my* father, he loves *me* and that I am *His* child! And that as His child I share in God's own life and that this new life is His Kingdom, which is growing within each of us.

This new awareness of the Kingdom of God has gradually been growing within me, I suppose, ever since Sarah first became ill and we realised that we couldn't manage on our own, and so turned to God. He responded to our cries for help and looking back over the last two years, I am filled with gratitude for the wonderful ways in which God has been revealing both His presence and His love to us. For Simon, the many 'thunderbolts' he received completely shattered the doubts that he had had and gave him a faith in God that he had never known before.

My faith, too, had been greatly strengthened. God had touched my life so deeply that I knew I had to respond. I just had to allow this new relationship to deepen and grow. I knew that I had to search for something more. And of course I didn't realise it at the time but this strong desire to know God more clearly and the need to deepen my relationship with Him, was all part of the action of the Holy Spirit. And it was His presence and His action in my life that I was to become increasingly more and more aware of, as my search progressed.

I suppose that in a way I felt as if I had come to the edge of the sea and although I had ventured in a little way, God was now asking me or prompting me to venture in deeper still but, in order to do so, I had to let go and jump! I needed to trust God and hand my life over to Him and allow Him to do the rest.

The Holy Spirit was not only prompting me to jump, He was also gently providing me with all the opportunities I needed in order to do so. And when I look back over this last year and see how God has been working in my life, I am again filled with gratitude at the beautiful way in which He has been leading me to a wonderful new awareness of His great love for us and of His presence in our lives. For me, this has been the most important and certainly one of the most wonderful discoveries of my life.

A few months after Sarah's death, I was asked by a friend if I wanted to join a Bible study group that was just starting. A group of about ten of us of mixed denominations met once a week, and together we read and reflected on the Bible. This was my first introduction to hearing and listening to the word of God with new meaning. A tremendous fellowship soon grew within the group as, in the light of the Gospels, we shared experiences, problems and worries together and re-examined our own lives. Our group soon became, for us all, a very important part of our week. God was definitely moving and working among us. His word was becoming flesh within us, giving our lives a new perspective and deeper meaning and also filling us with much joy and inner healing.

From July onwards, as we ourselves remembered so painfully the events of the preceding year, when Sarah had first become ill, I prayed even more that God would increase our trust in Him and that He would give us the strength to cope with our renewed feelings of grief.

Then very suddenly, at the end of September, we received the news that Father Cashin, our parish priest, was to be moved to another parish. I was shaken by this news and very upset. This first year after Sarah's death we had been so grateful for Father Cashin's presence and the thought of him leaving now, of all times, only shortly before our first Christmas without her and all that that would mean to us, reduced me to tears. But I was forgetting that God was in control of the situation and that He was simply asking me to place my hand in His and trust Him.

How quick I had been to forget, when faced with a situation that I didn't like, just what God had been showing us so well over the last year: that He is at our sides, that He does love us and that we can trust Him. Much later on I was to read, 'What father among you would hand his son a stone when he asked for bread?' (Matt. 7:9). And then I understood that God our Father can hand us only things that are good for us, because He loves us so much. And that when we ask for His help, He does help. Only sometimes what He seems to be handing us doesn't seem to us to be what we want or what we consider is good for us. And then I understood that very often God does hand us what seem to be stones: problems, sufferings, situations in our lives that we don't like or want, and we can't understand how our loving Father could allow these things to happen to us. We forget that He can hand us only bread, and the things in our lives which seem to us to be stones are only stones on the surface. Really they are gifts of love from our heavenly Father, things that can help us to grow closer to Him.

So, faced with this new situation, after my initial lack of trust, I started praising God instead. I praised Him for the fact that Father Cashin was leaving and that it was at this particular time in our lives. I praised Him for our new parish priest, whom we hadn't yet met. Little did I know then how very instrumental our new parish priest would be in helping to guide me towards this wonderful new awareness of God in my life. In praising God, I turned towards Him more and more, which I am sure is exactly what God wanted me to do. And as I turned towards Him, I found that although He knew everything about me, I knew very little about Him and now that He had touched my life so very deeply, it was important for me to find out more about Him, to give my relationship with Him a chance to grow.

And it was in prayer that I turned towards Him more and more. I was beginning to feel an increasing need for prayer and I started to try and find time to be with God on my own each day. The Mass was also becoming very important for me, and I started going to weekday Mass whenever I could. Prayer was changing. It wasn't just me talking to God any more but part of a real and growing relationship. Prayer was becoming more and more just being with God, becoming more aware of His presence and love and my unworthiness before Him. It was through prayer that I was becoming more aware of God's presence as Father, Son and Holy Spirit. It was through prayer that the Holy Spirit was going to start changing me, and through prayer that I started to hand myself over to Him. Praise was becoming more important and although I did often just talk to God, it was now becoming equally important to allow God to talk to me. I was also interested to know what God had said to other people, and what He had done in their lives. I suppose this is why I started reading religious books quite so avidly! However, more important than any of these for me was now the Bible, and now the Old Testament and the Psalms were for the first time becoming meaningful to me.

I also prayed that God would give me a deeper awareness of His presence in my life. He most certainly was doing that, except that to start with, at least, it was a very gradual process, and I wasn't aware that anything was happening. I joined the local prayer group which met at someone's house each week. To begin with, I found it difficult to share spontaneous prayer with other people. Prayer, for me, had previously always been either very private or else it had been public, as in church with set prayers. The idea of vocalised inner prayer was initially not easy. Gradually, however, I began to see how very beautiful prayer is, shared with a group of people, and how very powerful it is to praise and thank God together, to share what He is doing in our lives, to ask Him for the things we need and simply just to be with Him together and allow Him to speak through us. And not only was it very beautiful, it was also deepening my relationship with God.

In June, with a few others from the prayer group, I attended a charismatic day of renewal. This was a major turning point for me. At the time I knew very little about the charismatic renewal in the Catholic Church. I was to find out that it is a movement of the Holy Spirit within the Church and it is based on a new awareness and experience of the presence and the action of the Holy Spirit in one's life.

As a Catholic, I believe that Christians receive new life when they are baptised. This new life is, in fact, the life of the Holy Spirit, who comes to live within each of us. But for many people, this new life remains hidden and dormant. It certainly was for me. I was baptised as a tiny baby and although I was brought up as a Catholic and confirmed at the age of twelve, I was unaware of the wonderful life of the Spirit within me. It hadn't yet become a conscious experience for me. It needed to be reawakened, renewed, released more powerfully in my life. This reawakening, or new experience of the Holy Spirit's presence and action in one's life, is often referred to as 'Baptism in the Spirit' or sometimes as a 'new outpouring' of the Holy Spirit.

When this power is released, possibly suddenly or often over a longer period of time, it involves a change of heart for the person concerned and a new and deeper commitment to Jesus Christ as Lord of one's life. In other words, one consciously hands one's life over more and more to Jesus Christ.

It is often accompanied by a release of the gifts or *charisms* (hence the word 'charismatic') of the Holy Spirit, which are gifts not only for the individual, but gifts of service for the upbuilding and strengthening of the whole church, for the whole Body of Christ. Renewal also makes one realise that we need to allow the Holy Spirit to work within us. Our life as a Christian is not a matter of trying to do something on our own, but of co-operating with God and allowing Him to do something with us.

Although I was unaware of it at the time, I now realise that the Holy Spirit had already begun to renew me! And I gradually came to experience (and still am experiencing) this outpouring of the Holy Spirit. For it isn't a once and for all experience (for most people at least) but a continuous process of renewing. As we commit and recommit our lives each day to Jesus as Lord, the Holy Spirit gradually transforms us and the new life within us grows, so that with our co-operation we become the potential Christ-like person that God wants us to be.

My growing awareness of the presence of God in my life and the wonderful new vision of God that I experienced on that first day of renewal overwhelmed me! I was so full of the love and joy and peace of the Lord that I came home and hardly slept all night. I lay awake and praised God for such a wonderful experience!

A few months later, I attended a five-day conference of renewal and again I was overwhelmed by the love and joy and peace that I experienced. But more than the wonderful fellowship, the inspiring talks, the beautiful Masses and the fantastic singing, I just felt incredibly privileged to have experienced a new vision of the Kingdom of God that is with us here and now: a vision of God's love for us that is so much clearer than ever before. And it is so wonderful that I want to shout out *alleluia* and tell everyone that God loves us and wants to share His life with us now, this very minute. No matter what we've done, God loves us; we are His children, He is our Father. Our God loves us so much that not only did He become a man and die for us, He has sent us the Holy Spirit, who lives, works and breathes within our very beings. What a fantastic thought, so fantastic that we can't begin to grasp it! God Himself wants to live in us, love in us, and work in us, and through the Holy Spirit, He is renewing and will renew the face of the earth: His Kingdom is growing on earth for it is growing within each one of us!

Before the renewal had come into my life, I thought that I had to try to do something for God. I didn't realise, as I do now, that I can't do anything for God unless I allow God to do something for me and He does that by the action of the Holy Spirit. And it is fantastic to see what the Holy Spirit has been doing to me! It's as if my eyes and my ears and my whole being have suddenly become alive! And for the first time, I am able to see, able to hear!

Suddenly the Bible seems to be jumping out at me and for the first time in my life I realise that it *is* the word of God! God really is talking to *me*! And He wants me to listen to what He is saying and let His word become flesh in me. Not only has the Bible become more alive for me, but everything is taking on a new meaning! I praise God for the smallest things as well as for the big things; in fact, everyday routine things have become more important, as I realise that they, too, are part of God's gift of love to me. I am conscious of the presence of God in everything around me and especially in the countryside, in a way I have never felt before, and I praise Him for His presence even when it is pouring with rain or very windy! Things which I would once probably have grumbled about I am now praising God for!

The Mass and the sacraments, too, have all become alive and so much more meaningful to me and I seem to be hearing and understanding the words of the Mass for the very first time. Above all, they have become wonderful celebrations of God's great love for us. I just seem to be so much more aware of His incredible love for me! My God loves me, exactly as I am, with all my faults, with all my sins and He has chosen me personally, by name, to be His own daughter!

When I started to realise this, I also became aware that some action was needed on my part. If God was calling me to be His daughter, I needed to respond to His invitation. I needed to respond to Jesus Christ when He says 'Follow me!' And then I realised that, yes, I wanted to follow Him, wherever He wanted me to go, whatever He wanted me to do. I wanted to follow Him with my whole heart, with my whole self, with my whole life. I wanted Jesus Christ to be Lord of my life! I wanted to place my life in His hands and trust Him and let Him lead me. I wanted Him to transform me with His love and fill me more and more with His own life. But to do so, he needs to chip away at all those bits of me that are not of Him. I need to be broken, so that the Holy Spirit can transform me, and the Christ-like person within me, the person God wants me to be, can be released.

As I have become more aware of God's love for me I have, at the same time, become increasingly aware of my own sinfulness, my own total unworthiness before God. And more and more I realise that I am in need of His mercy, His forgiveness, His healing and His strength. And I am sure this is why the Sacrament of Reconciliation (as we now call the Sacrament of Penance, or Confession), has become so much more important for me and through this beautiful sacrament, I have experienced great peace, great love, great joy and also deep inner healing.

I feel so grateful for this incredible new experience of the Holy Spirit's presence and action in my life and I thank God with all my heart for this wonderful new awareness of His love for me and for the beautiful new vision of the kingdom of God that I have been, and still am, experiencing. But it is not just for me, but for everyone! And what's more it is a free gift! It doesn't matter what we've done, what is important is that God loves us. And He wants us to turn to Him, He wants to give us His strength, He wants to turn our sorrow into joy, He wants to share His love and His life with each one of us. And if we turn to Him and really want to find Him, then we *will* find Him. I pray that if you have not yet found God, you will ask Him to show you that He is there and He does love you. And having found Him, say 'yes' to Him, for when we say 'yes', then He is able to work in us and the new life He gives us can grow, and His kingdom will come.

Simon and I have so many gifts to thank God for, and Sarah is one of them. Her life was a very precious gift and we have many happy memories of her short nine years. But her death, too, was a gift: a gift, because in the depth of our grief we have found God, a God who loves us, who walks with us, and who dwells within us.

Sarah trusted God. In spite of her illness and all her suffering, she very simply accepted that God loved her and in doing so, she allowed God to transform her with His love and fill her with His life, which shone from her quite visibly just before she died. The Kingdom of God grew within her because she had no barriers, as we adults often have. She just accepted quietly and simply everything that was happening to her. And because of this, she was completely open to the action of the Holy Spirit, for her quiet acceptance was also her unconditional 'yes' to what God wanted to do for her and in her.

Just as Sarah allowed the Kingdom of God to grow within her, we too must place our trust in our heavenly Father; we too, must be like little children and allow our loving Father to carry us in His arms, knowing that if we trust Him it doesn't matter what is happening to us, for His love is stronger than anything there is. And He will also give us His strength, and the more we trust Him, the more we allow Him to build up His Kingdom of love within us.

So, with His help, we will continue to praise and thank Him for everything, knowing that He loves us and is beside us all the way, and that He will lead us and guide us and renew us with His love, and bring us one day to be with Him in Heaven, as Sarah now is, filled with His love, filled with His peace, filled with His joy, to praise Him and thank Him for ever.

It would seem strange perhaps to choose a triumphant hymn proclaiming good news, peace and happiness, as a final hymn at a child's funeral service. But that is exactly what we did choose. It seemed right at the time and even more so now. For we were celebrating the fact that our God does indeed reign over everything, that His love is greater than anything that we could ever imagine and that because of His incredible love for us, death no longer has any power. For our God has visited His people; His message of peace and

love and happiness is Good News. For our God is still with
us, His kingdom is growing within us, His Holy Spirit is
moving and working throughout the world. We are being
made new.

> *How lovely on the mountains are the feet of Him*
> *Who brings good news, good news,*
> *Announcing peace, proclaiming news of happiness,*
> *Our God reigns, Our God reigns!*

THE TORN VEIL

Sister Gulshan and Thelma Sangster

Gulshan Fatima was brought up in a Muslim Sayed family according to the orthodox Islamic code of the Shias.
Suffering from a crippling paralysis she travelled to England in search of medical help. Although unsuccessful in medical terms, this trip marked the beginning of a spiritual awakening that led ultimately to her conversion to Christianity.
Gulshan and her father also travelled to Mecca in the hope that God would heal her, but that trip too was of no avail. However, Gulshan was not detered. She relentlessly pursued God and He faithfully answered her prayers. Her conversion, when it came, was dramatic and brought with a miraculous healing.
The Torn Veil is Sister Gulshan's thrilling testimony to the power of God which can break through every barrier.

If you wish to receive *regular information* about *new books*, please send your name and address to:

London Bible Warehouse
PO Box 123
Basingstoke
Hants RG23 7NL

Name ____

Address ____

____

____

____

I am especially interested in:
- ☐ Biographies
- ☐ Fiction
- ☐ Christian living
- ☐ Issue related books
- ☐ Academic books
- ☐ Bible study aids
- ☐ Children's books
- ☐ Music
- ☐ Other subjects

P.S. If you have ideas for new Christian Books or other products, please write to us too!